INSIDE OUTSIDE

A Behind the Scenes Look at Kentucky Basketball

A Behind the Scenes   Look at Kentucky Basketball

Copyright© 1995 by Host Communications

"Inside/Outside: A Behind the Scenes Look at Kentucky Basketball" is published and printed by Host Communications, 904 North Broadway, Lexington, Kentucky 40505. W. James Host, Publisher, Richard A. Ford, Associate Publisher, Eric Barnhart, Director of Publishing.

Photography by Brian Spurlock. Photos of Kentucky-Arizona State game provided by Doug DeVoe
Written by Tom Wallace
Edited by David Kaplan
Cover design and layout by Jamie Barker
Marketing and distribution by Kim Ramsay, Dani Clore
Editorial assistance by Dave Mrvos, Mike Nayman, Jai Giffin, Craig Baroncelli, Pat Henderson, Dan Peters, Jim Kelsey, Mark Buerger, Jared Svoboda, Randy O'Neal, Will Roleson, Mark Coyle, Stacey Durbin Gish, Judy Grossman, Jay Stubblefield, Michael Wakefield
Design assistance by Paulette Ball, Laura Doolittle, Dana Bart, Stephen Tutt, Tammi Geierman

ISBN: 1-879688-86-7

INSIDE OUTSIDE

A Behind the Scenes **Look at Kentucky Basketball**

Table of Contents

I'm a Kentuckian by birth; if not, I would have been one by choice. By the same token I am a Kentucky Wildcat fan. Since I can remember, I have followed the fortunes of the Wildcats. As a small boy, I followed their feats through the voices of J.B. Faulconer and Claude Sullivan. As a young man, I did the same through the voice and eyes of Cawood Ledford. Like the young people of today, my room was filled with mementos of the Cats.

Like most boys growing up in Kentucky, I dreamed of playing for the Cats. Like most, that dream never would become a reality. What did become a reality was the dream of getting to travel with the Cats. Becoming friends with the coaches. Getting to see them as people, not just as names and numbers. Learning of their lives both on and off the floor.

The following pages provide for you the opportunity to witness in pictures and words the season that produced a Southeastern Conference regular season championship. The heartbreaking loss to defending national champion Arkansas, in Fayetteville, and the win over the Razorbacks for the SEC Tournament championship and a trip to the NCAA Southeast regional championship game. You will see the Wildcats at home and on the road, in practice and in the game. You will see them as they were, 13 young men and a coaching staff striving to deliver a championship program for the university, and a multitude of fans from border to border and coast to coast.

In short, you will see them Inside/Outside.

Enjoy.

Ralph Hacker
University of Kentucky Broadcaster

Foreword

A Behind the Scenes   Look at Kentucky Basketball

The dual purpose of this book is to give fans a permanent record of the 1994-95 UK basketball season and to take them behind the scenes with the Wildcats. I think we've succeeded, thanks mainly to the truly extraordinary photography of Brian Spurlock. Brian was given total access to the players and coaches at home and on the road, and the result is a rare glimpse at what it's like to be a Kentucky Wildcat.

Doing a book is never easy, but thanks to the cooperation of the players, coaches and the rest of the support personnel, this project turned out to be an enjoyable one for me. In particular, I would like to thank Rick Pitino and Jim O'Brien for tolerating me at practice and for answering the million questions I had for them. Their patience was infinite.

Tom Wallace
4/17/95

Introduction

THE SEASON

1994 Nov. 9 Rupp Arena • Lexington, Ky.

Athletes in Action 86
Kentucky 122

"Who designed our new uniforms? Well, that depends. If the fans like them, then Rick will take the credit. But if the fans don't like them, like last year, then you can bet he'll lay the blame on me."

— Bill Keightley

Junior Walter McCarty and freshman Antoine Walker combined for 51 points off the bench as the Wildcats pounded Athletes in Action 122-86 in an exhibition game at Rupp Arena. McCarty, pressed into early duty at the pivot position when Andre Riddick went down with a knee injury less than two minutes into the game, made good on 11 of 19 field goal attempts en route to a 30-point performance. He also grabbed 11 rebounds. Walker, the smooth 6-8 Chicago native, finished with 21 points in his Wildcat debut. Other Cats in double figures were Tony Delk (18), Jared Prickett (16) and Rodrick Rhodes (13). Prickett led all rebounders with 15. The Cats won easily despite being at less than full strength. Mark Pope's long-awaited debut was put on hold because of a knee injury, while senior Chris Harrison missed the game

because of a broken bone in his right hand. In addition, freshman Scott Padgett sat out because of academic troubles. Still, the game was never in doubt, thanks mainly to the Cats' full-court pressure and their dominance on the boards. Kentucky forced Athletes in Action into 25 turnovers and won the

rebounding battle 56-35. Success with the press translated into a host of easy shots, which explains why the Cats hit 52.9 percent from the field. UK did experience problems in one area — cramping. At one point, Delk, McCarty and Rhodes were on the bench being treated for leg cramps.

Athletes in Action	fg-a	3-pt	ft-a	rb	a	b	pf	tp
Cheyanne Gibson	4-8	1-3	1-3	4	2	0	2	10
Robert Sewell	3-6	2-3	3-3	3	1	0	5	11
Mike Ravizee	5-12	0-0	3-7	12	1	1	2	13
Rod Foster	7-11	2-5	2-2	1	1	0	1	18
Ryan Yoder	1-3	1-3	5-5	3	4	0	1	8
Milton Banks	4-11	0-0	2-3	3	2	1	3	10
Emory Lewis	2-6	0-0	0-0	3	0	1	1	4
David Daniels	1-4	0-0	3-4	0	5	0	3	5
Dave Heidebrecht	2-5	0-1	0-0	4	0	0	5	4
Ed Uszynski	1-5	1-2	0-0	0	2	0	0	3
Team rebounds				2				
Totals	**30-71**	**7-17**	**19-27**	**35**	**18**	**3**	**23**	**86**

Kentucky	fg-a	3-pt	ft-a	rb	a	b	pf	tp
Rodrick Rhodes	6-9	0-0	1-2	2	5	1	2	13
Jared Prickett	7-11	0-0	2-7	15	4	0	3	16
Andre Riddick	0-1	0-0	0-0	2	1	0	0	0
Tony Delk	8-11	2-3	0-0	6	4	0	1	18
Jeff Sheppard	3-8	1-1	2-2	7	4	0	4	9
Walter McCarty	11-19	2-6	6-9	11	5	5	4	30
Anthony Epps	2-5	1-4	0-0	2	3	0	2	5
Antoine Walker	6-17	2-5	7-8	8	4	3	3	21
Allen Edwards	1-3	0-2	2-2	1	1	1	4	4
Cameron Mills	2-3	2-2	0-0	1	1	0	0	6
Team rebounds				1				
Totals	**46-87**	**10-23**	**20-30**	**56**	**32**	**10**	**23**	**122**

Athletes in Action	39	47	—	86
Kentucky	60	62	—	122

Turnovers: Athletes in Action 25, Kentucky 19
Technicals: none
Officials: David Bair, Curtis Shaw, Bruce Benedict
Attendance: 21,695

KENTUCKY

Lithuanian Nationals   **81**
Kentucky   **114**

Freshman Antoine Walker continued his impressive play, scoring a team-best 22 points as the Cats geared up for the regular campaign by easily defeating the Lithuanian National team 114-81. Once again, UK's full-court press proved to be the difference, forcing the visitors into 34 turnovers. That stat was more than enough to offset the one area where the Cats were whipped — rebounding. Lithuania won the battle of the boards 40-39. The Cats struggled early, bothered somewhat by Lithuania's superior size inside, but once the press began to take its toll, the outcome was quickly decided. UK led 56-42 at intermission, and thanks to 62 percent shooting in the second half, never looked back. Tony Delk added 19 points to the Cats' coffers, while Walter McCarty and Rhodes had 18 and 16, respectively. McCarty completed a "double-double" by pulling down 10 rebounds.

Sophomore point guard Anthony Epps also turned in a superb effort, handing out 14 assists while committing only one turnover. The game also marked the long-awaited debut of Mark Pope, the much-heralded 6-9 junior pivot man who sat out last season after transferring from Washington, where he was the Pac-10 Freshman of the Year in 1991-92. Pope finished with seven points in his first game as a Wildcat. Andre Riddick, who was feared to be lost for an extended time because of a knee injury sustained during UK's first exhibition game, scored seven points and blocked three shots.

"We still have a long way to go, but you can see the potential out there. I'm very impressed with the potential of this team. They have fun and play together well. The chemistry is good."

— Rick Pitino

Lithuanian Nat.	fg-a	3-pt	ft-a	rb	a	b	pf	tp
S. Strombergas	5-7	1-2	2-4	5	2	0	5	13
G. Einikis	6-14	0-0	5-8	5	3	2	2	17
Z. Ilgauskas	11-21	0-0	4-6	19	1	4	3	26
D. Sirtautas	3-10	0-4	0-0	3	2	0	1	6
D. Lukminas	3-7	0-4	0-0	2	6	0	2	6
V. Jurgilas	3-4	2-3	0-2	3	1	0	4	8
R. Vaisvilas	1-1	1-1	1-2	0	3	0	1	4
K. Kemzura	0-0	0-0	1-2	0	0	0	0	1
N. Zabarauskas	0-0	0-0	0-0	1	0	0	0	0
Team rebounds				2				
Totals	**32-64**	**4-14**	**13-24**	**40**	**18**	**6**	**18**	**81**

Kentucky	fg-a	3-pt	ft-a	rb	a	b	pf	tp
Rodrick Rhodes	8-16	0-1	0-1	5	2	0	2	16
Walter McCarty	7-14	1-4	3-3	10	2	0	2	18
Jared Prickett	1-4	0-0	0-1	5	1	0	3	2
Andre Riddick	3-4	0-0	1-2	2	0	3	0	7
Tony Delk	7-9	2-4	3-3	1	2	0	3	19
Jeff Sheppard	4-6	0-1	0-0	2	1	0	0	8
Mark Pope	2-5	1-1	2-2	1	1	0	5	7
Anthony Epps	4-7	1-4	0-0	1	14	0	1	9
Antoine Walker	8-15	3-4	3-5	7	4	0	3	22
Allen Edwards	3-5	0-0	0-0	0	2	0	2	6
Cameron Mills	0-1	0-1	0-0	0	0	0	0	0
Scott Padgett	0-2	0-2	0-0	1	0	0	1	0
Team rebounds				2				
Totals	**47-88**	**8-22**	**12-17**	**39**	**29**	**3**	**22**	**114**

Lithuanian Nationals	42	39	—	81
Kentucky	56	58	—	114

Turnovers: Lithuania 34, Kentucky 14
Technicals: none
Officials: John Clougherty, David Bair, Tom Eades
Attendance: 22,897

1994

Nov. 26

Rupp Arena • Lexington, Ky.

UT-Martin	50
Kentucky	124

"There's not much you can say about a game like this. Our opponent played hard, but they were clearly overmatched as far as size and quickness."

— Rick Pitino

I n a mismatch that Sitting Bull would have appreciated, the Cats kicked off the 1994-95 season by rolling to a ridiculously easy 124-50 win over UT-Martin. The 74-point margin was just three shy of UK's all-time winning point spread, which came in a 144-66 win over Georgia in 1956. The margin was, however, great enough to break two records — UK's most lopsided win during Rick Pitino's six years as head coach and its biggest romp in the 19-year history of Rupp Arena. Both previous marks came in Kentucky's 101-40 clubbing of Tennessee during the 1993 SEC Tournament. After the two clubs exchanged early buckets, the Cats went on a 25-2 run that quickly turned the game into a yawner. By the half, the Cats were leading 62-24. As was the case in the two exhibition games, UK's press proved to be the difference. UT-Martin, blind-sided from every angle, turned the ball

over on 42 occasions, many of which led to uncontested Wildcat buckets. So efficient was the Cats' thievery that they managed to tie the school record of 23 steals. In particular, forward Jared Prickett, who led the Cats in scoring with 21 points, made good on 10 of 11 field goal attempts. Six other Cats

cracked double figures, including Tony Delk (17), Rodrick Rhodes (16), Antoine Walker (15), Andre Riddick (11), Mark Pope (11) and Walter McCarty (10). All Cats who saw action scored. The win represented the sixth consecutive opening game triumph for Kentucky, all under Pitino.

"A blast.
Tonight was
a definite blast."

— Jared Prickett

Tennessee-Martin	fg-a	3-pt	ft-a	rb	a	b	pf	tp
Michael Hart	7-15	0-0	2-2	4	0	0	1	16
Gregor Bojovic	0-1	0-0	0-0	1	1	0	4	0
Ryan Burge	1-4	0-0	2-2	4	0	0	4	4
DeWayne Powell	3-7	1-4	5-8	2	3	0	1	12
Demarko Wright	2-4	1-1	0-0	3	2	0	0	5
Chris Busyn	2-3	0-0	1-1	3	1	0	5	5
Jim Locum	0-3	0-3	0-0	4	2	0	2	0
B.J. Nelson	1-1	0-0	0-0	1	0	0	2	2
Vennie Sherrod	0-3	0-2	0-0	0	0	0	0	0
Robin Cude	2-2	2-2	0-0	0	0	0	0	6
Team rebounds				2				
Totals	18-43	4-12	10-13	24	9	0	19	50

Kentucky	fg-a	3-pt	ft-a	rb	a	b	pf	tp
Rodrick Rhodes	6-17	2-2	2-4	3	7	0	2	16
Walter McCarty	5-7	0-1	0-1	6	1	1	3	10
Jared Prickett	10-11	0-0	1-1	8	1	0	2	21
Andre Riddick	5-6	0-0	1-1	8	0	3	1	11
Tony Delk	7-12	3-5	0-0	2	3	0	2	17
Jeff Sheppard	1-5	1-2	4-4	1	3	0	1	7
Mark Pope	3-4	0-0	5-6	7	1	0	4	11
Anthony Epps	0-2	0-1	3-4	0	7	0	0	3
Antoine Walker	6-13	0-3	3-3	2	0	0	0	15
Allen Edwards	2-2	1-1	1-2	0	1	0	2	6
Cameron Mills	2-3	1-1	2-2	2	3	0	0	7
Team rebounds				1				
Totals	47-82	8-16	22-28	40	27	4	17	124

Tennessee-Martin 24	26	—	50
Kentucky 62	62	—	124

Turnovers: Tennessee-Martin 42, Kentucky 8
Technicals: none
Officials: André Pattillo, Gene Monje, Tony Greene
Attendance: 23,785

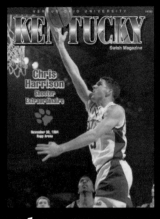

KENTUCKY Swish Magazine
Chris Harrison
Shooter Extraordinaire

1994

Nov. 30

Rupp Arena • Lexington, Ky.

Ohio U.	**74**
Kentucky	**79**

"Great post defense starts with pressure on the ball. You cannot play Gary Trent one on one. You need incredible heat on the ball and weak-side help. We played phenomenal defense tonight."

— Rick Pitino

"We had them on the ropes, because we had momentum. They hadn't been in that situation. I told the guys, let's get the lead and see how they handle it."

— (Ohio U. coach) Larry Hunter

After three easy blow-out victories, UK coach Rick Pitino finally got what he wanted — a war. Pitino said his troops needed testing before taking on UCLA and Indiana, and that's precisely what happened, courtesy of a disciplined, tenacious Ohio University club fresh off winning the Preseason NIT. The Cats watched as a 14-point second-half lead was whittled down to one with just more than three minutes remaining, then used timely defense in clutch situations and excellent free throw shooting to avoid an upset. Leading 66-65, Rodrick Rhodes hit one of two free throws and a short jumper to give UK a 69-65 advantage. Kentucky's defense forced Ohio's Geno Ford into a rushed shot, which missed and was rebounded by Walter McCarty. Mark Pope dropped in a pair of free throws, the first of five freebies he would make inside the final 1:08. McCarty and Anthony Epps also sank two free throws

each to help seal the victory. The outstanding defensive effort by both clubs is reflected in their respective shooting percentages — UK shot 37.9, Ohio 37.7. UK, which opened by hitting just one of its first 15 field goal attempts, trailed by as many as seven points in the first half, and had the Cats not scored on 14 of their final 19 possessions before

intermission, they might have found themselves in too deep a hole to climb out of. It was, Pitino later pointed out, defense that enabled UK to avoid disaster. McCarty and Jared Prickett received high praise from Pitino for the job they did on Ohio's great Gary Trent, who scored 21 points, but made just six of 17 from the field.

Ohio University	fg-a	3-pt	ft-a	rb	a	b	pf	tp
Gary Trent	6-17	0-2	9-11	10	2	0	3	21
Jeff Boals	1-4	0-1	3-4	4	2	0	4	5
Jason Terry	0-2	0-0	0-0	2	1	1	3	0
Geno Ford	5-11	0-2	7-8	2	2	0	3	17
Gus Johnson	3-7	3-5	8-9	4	0	0	2	17
Curtis Simmons	1-5	0-0	1-2	8	0	0	4	3
Ed Sears	1-3	0-0	0-0	3	0	1	0	2
Mike Reese	3-4	1-1	2-2	1	1	0	5	9
Ryan Greenwood	0-0	0-0	0-0	0	0	0	0	0
Team rebounds				2				
Totals	**20-53**	**4-11**	**30-36**	**36**	**8**	**2**	**24**	**74**

Kentucky	fg-a	3-pt	ft-a	rb	a	b	pf	tp
Rodrick Rhodes	3-12	1-1	2-4	2	5	1	2	9
Walter McCarty	6-12	1-3	4-5	9	2	1	3	17
Jared Prickett	2-6	0-1	4-6	8	3	1	2	8
Andre Riddick	0-0	0-0	0-0	2	0	0	3	0
Tony Delk	7-11	2-3	1-2	2	1	1	2	17
Anthony Epps	4-9	2-6	5-5	1	0	0	2	15
Mark Pope	2-7	0-1	7-8	11	0	1	4	11
Allen Edwards	0-0	0-0	0-0	1	2	0	3	0
Antoine Walker	0-7	0-1	0-0	3	2	0	3	0
Jeff Sheppard	1-2	0-1	0-0	1	1	0	2	2
Scott Padgett	0-0	0-0	0-0	0	0	0	0	0
Team rebounds				2				
Totals	**25-66**	**6-17**	**23-30**	**42**	**16**	**5**	**26**	**79**

Ohio University	32	42	—	74
Kentucky	41	38	—	79

Turnovers: Ohio University 15, Kentucky 10
Technicals: none
Officials: Don Rutledge, Les Jones, Bennie Adams
Attendance: 24, 212

Australia, Hawaii, Alaska, Japan, Israel ... those are just a few of the more exotic locales where University of Kentucky basketball teams have played. And Italy will be added to this list in August of '95. Travel has always been an integral part of UK basketball. As one of the most successful and illustrious programs of all time, UK is in demand around the globe. Because of that, Wildcat players have been afforded the opportunity to go places and see things that they otherwise might never get a chance to. Those are lifetime experiences that stay with the players long after the games have ended and the sound of the cheers has faded away. It's the part of an education that can't be taught in a classroom. Down through the years, almost every UK team has played in at least one memorable location. This year, for instance, it was Southern California for the John R. Wooden Classic. Next season,

it's Manhattan, for a second appearance in four years in the Holiday Festival. And, of course, in between there's the two-week trip to Italy for an exhibition tour. What makes these trips special is the opportunity for the players to visit such disparate shrines as Disneyland and the Vatican and to meet such icons as the Pope and Mickey Mouse. When UK takes a trip, such as the one to California, there are approximately 50 people in the entourage. In addition, because of Kentucky's incredible support, there are literally hundreds of fans who make the pilgrimage. For the California trip, four different charter planes were available for fans wishing to follow the team. Already, a plan is available for fans who want to make the trip to Italy. Kentucky players are fortunate in many ways, and nowhere is that more true than when it comes to traveling. That part of the college experience is priceless.

DISNEY
The Wildcats Invade

JOHN R. WOODEN Classic

The Inaugural

JOHN R. WOODEN Classic

Saturday, December 3, 1994

The Pond of Anaheim

1994

Dec. 3

The Pond • Anaheim, Calif

Kentucky 81
UCLA 82

"We didn't do a good job of taking care of the basketball at the end of the game. We put ourselves into a position to win the game, then we failed to execute. That's something we need to work on."

— Rick Pitino

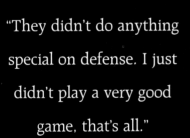

"They didn't do anything special on defense. I just didn't play a very good game, that's all."

— Tony Delk

I t was a meeting between two of college basketball's true titans — tradition-rich and hardware-heavy UK and UCLA (owners of a combined 16 NCAA titles) in the inaugural John R. Wooden Classic. And it didn't disappoint. The Bruins, thanks to a gritty comeback late in the game, used two free throws by freshman J.R. Henderson to edge the Cats 82-81. In order to secure the win, UCLA had to overcome an eight-point UK lead in the final four minutes. Despite the Bruins' late charge, it appeared as if the Cats were going to hang on for the win when Rodrick Rhodes' jumper gave them an 81-78 lead with 44.9 seconds remaining. Even after UCLA's George Zidek hit a hook shot to slice the difference to a single point, all the Cats had to do to escape with the win was run out the clock or force the Bruins to foul. Instead, the Cats threw the ball away, which gave UCLA

one final shot at winning. Henderson, taking a feed from point guard Tyus Edney, drove for the bucket and drew a foul from Walter McCarty. Or did he? McCarty and his coach, Rick Pitino, thought otherwise, arguing that McCarty got only ball. Henderson said McCarty got the ball — and body. The official agreed with

Henderson, who went to the line and hit the game-winners. UK controlled the game throughout, leading 38-33 at the half and by 10 with eight minutes left despite a nightmare game from leading scorer Tony Delk. Early foul problems rendered him ineffective. Rhodes, however, played his finest game of the young season, scoring 16 points.

Kentucky	fg-a	3-pt	ft-a	rb	a	b	pf	tp
Rodrick Rhodes	5-13	2-3	4-4	4	4	0	4	16
Walter McCarty	5-8	2-3	0-0	6	1	0	5	12
Mark Pope	2-4	0-0	8-8	8	2	0	1	12
Tony Delk	3-7	0-2	1-2	2	0	0	5	7
Anthony Epps	4-8	1-3	3-5	5	4	0	0	12
Chris Harrison	0-1	0-1	0-0	0	0	0	0	0
Andre Riddick	0-0	0-0	0-0	0	0	0	0	0
Jeff Sheppard	4-8	1-2	5-6	2	1	0	2	14
Allen Edwards	0-1	0-0	0-0	0	0	0	1	0
Antoine Walker	2-9	0-2	3-5	4	0	1	4	7
Jared Prickett	0-4	0-1	1-3	8	1	1	4	1
Team rebounds				1				
Totals	25-63	6-17	25-33	40	13	2	26	81

UCLA	fg-a	3-pt	ft-a	rb	a	b	pf	tp
Charles O'Bannon	4-13	0-1	4-4	3	0	0	5	12
Ed O'Bannon	9-17	2-6	6-11	6	2	2	2	26
George Zidek	7-11	0-0	2-5	10	0	1	4	16
Cameron Dollar	1-3	0-1	0-2	3	3	0	3	2
Tyus Edney	4-7	2-3	3-4	7	5	0	4	13
Marquis Burns	0-3	0-1	0-0	0	1	0	0	0
Toby Bailey	0-2	0-1	1-2	2	1	0	3	1
omm'A Givens	1-2	0-0	0-0	0	0	0	0	2
J.R. Henderson	1-3	0-1	8-8	4	2	1	4	10
Team rebounds				4				
Totals	27-59	4-14	24-36	39	14	4	25	82

Kentucky	38	43 —	81
UCLA	33	49 —	82

Turnovers: Kentucky 19, UCLA 18
Technicals: Kentucky — Pitino
Officials: Ed Hightower, Gerry Donahy, David Hall
Attendance: 18,307

THE
INDIANA-
KENTUCKY
GAME

December 7, 1994
Freedom Hall
Louisville, KY

Alan Henderson   Tony Delk

1994 Dec. 7

Freedom Hall • Louisville, Ky.

Indiana   70
Kentucky   73

"I was positive the game would be played this way, that it would be two or three points either way. It was a great, great game, and I'm very excited that we won."

— Rick Pitino

"What kind of a shot were we looking for at the end? We wanted a guy at the top of the key with no one within 20 feet of him."

— Bob Knight

Defense ruled this game, played before a packed house in Louisville's Freedom Hall. Every move was contested, every shot was challenged. It was typical Bob Knight versus Rick Pitino, and it was good stuff from start to finish. So tough was the defense that UK didn't score in the final 1:37, while IU went the final three minutes without scoring a bucket. UK prevailed by doing precisely what it failed to do in the loss to UCLA — execute down the stretch. After leading 33-30 at intermission, UK fell behind 47-41 early in the second half. Only seconds later, a three-point play by Tony Delk and a trey by Anthony Epps tied it at 49-49 with 9:46 remaining. With IU on top 64-62, freshman Neil Reed was hit with a technical foul. Epps sank two free throws to knot the score once again. UK went in front for good at the 3:08

mark when Delk posted up for a three-point play. Then McCarty hit from deep in the left corner to make it 73-69. Reed, the sensational rookie point guard, hit one of two freebies with 1:20 left. After McCarty missed two free throws, Reed's last three-pointer was off the mark. McCarty led UK with 16 points. Delk, who suffered through another tough

shooting night (5 of 19), had 11, while Rodrick Rhodes and Antoine Walker each chipped in with 10. Reed and Brian Evans led IU with 17 apiece. The low shooting percentages reflected the defensive intensity. IU shot 45 percent, UK 38.9. IU easily won the rebounding battle, 47-31. UK's victory evened Pitino's record against Knight at 3-3.

Indiana	fg-a	3-pt	ft-a	rb	a	b	pf	tp
Brian Evans	6-12	0-3	5-7	9	3	1	3	17
Alan Henderson	7-14	0-0	2-3	8	1	4	5	16
Andrae Patterson	4-11	0-0	2-3	12	1	1	3	10
Neil Reed	5-11	2-5	5-7	1	3	0	1	17
Steve Hart	2-8	0-0	0-0	6	3	1	1	4
Pat Knight	0-1	0-1	0-0	0	2	0	0	0
Charlie Miller	2-2	0-0	0-0	0	0	0	0	4
Todd Lindeman	1-1	0-0	0-0	2	0	0	1	2
Team rebounds				9				
Totals	27-60	2-9	14-20	47	13	7	14	70

Kentucky	fg-a	3-pt	ft-a	rb	a	b	pf	tp
Rodrick Rhodes	5-14	0-5	0-0	0	3	1	5	10
Walter McCarty	4-9	4-8	4-6	4	1	1	2	16
Mark Pope	3-5	0-0	1-2	7	0	0	3	7
Tony Delk	5-19	0-7	1-2	3	5	0	1	11
Anthony Epps	1-3	1-3	4-4	1	4	0	2	7
Jeff Sheppard	3-6	0-1	0-0	0	1	0	2	6
Jared Prickett	3-5	0-0	0-0	6	0	2	5	6
Antoine Walker	4-10	2-4	0-0	5	0	2	2	10
Andre Riddick	0-0	0-0	0-0	0	0	0	0	0
Chris Harrison	0-1	0-0	0-0	0	1	0	0	0
Team rebounds				5				
Totals	28-72	7-28	10-14	31	15	6	22	73

Indiana	30	40	—	70
Kentucky	33	40	—	73

Turnovers: Indiana 24, Kentucky 13
Technicals: Indiana — Reed
Officials: Jim Burr, John Clougherty, Tom O'Neill
Attendance: 19,825

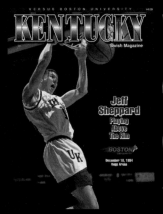

1994

Dec. 10

Rupp Arena • Lexington, Ky.

Boston U.	49
Kentucky	90

"It was not the type of game I thought it would be. On film, they looked good. I think they were overwhelmed by the size of this place. It was a whole new experience for them."

— Rick Pitino

A 13-0 run right out of the gate paved the way for the Cats' easy win over Rick Pitino's former place of employment. Mark Pope started UK's early explosion by knocking down his first three-point basket. A Pope dunk, a short jumper by Tony Delk and back-to-back Delk treys extended UK's lead to 13-0 less than three minutes into the game. The Terriers, unable to make any impression on the Cats' press, finally scored when Tunji Awojobi sank a three-pointer at the 16:04 mark. By then, Pitino had already begun substituting freely. Every UK player saw action in the first half, which ended with the Cats owning a commanding 50-21 lead. The second half featured less than sterling play by both clubs. Combined, the two teams managed to commit 50 turnovers — BU 26, UK 24. But UK's pressure defense was of such force that the Terriers never were able to take advantage of the Cats' sloppy play. For the game, BU made good on just 17 of 63 field goal attempts for 27 percent. UK shot well, hitting 31 of 60 attempts from the field. The Cats were equally efficient from three-point land, knocking down 11 of 25 trey attempts. Delk and freshman Antoine Walker led UK's scoring with 13 points apiece. Anthony Epps and Rodrick Rhodes also hit double digits with 11 and 10, respectively. Tremain Byrd's 14 points led BU.

Boston University	fg-a	3-pt	ft-a	rb	a	b	pf	tp
Tunji Awojobi	4-16	1-2	3-4	6	1	3	3	12
Steve Ehretsman	2-6	1-3	4-5	2	1	0	3	9
Dave Stiff	3-7	0-0	3-6	5	1	1	5	9
David Wallace	0-2	0-2	0-0	1	0	0	2	0
James Schwartz	0-1	0-0	0-0	3	0	0	0	0
Tremain Byrd	6-15	2-7	0-0	4	1	0	0	14
Raja Bell	1-6	0-1	1-2	1	0	0	2	3
B.J. Fearrington	0-3	0-1	0-0	2	3	0	3	0
Yusef Delayeffitte	0-1	0-0	0-0	0	0	0	5	0
John Brennan	1-4	0-1	0-0	3	0	0	1	2
Kenny Hubbard	0-1	0-1	0-0	0	0	0	0	0
Jim Whalen	0-1	0-0	0-0	0	0	0	1	0
Team rebounds				7				
Totals	**17-63**	**4-18**	**11-17**	**34**	**7**	**4**	**25**	**49**

Kentucky	fg-a	3-pt	ft-a	rb	a	b	pf	tp
Rodrick Rhodes	4-8	0-1	2-2	6	4	1	2	10
Walter McCarty	3-5	0-1	0-1	4	2	3	2	6
Mark Pope	2-4	1-1	2-2	5	0	1	1	7
Tony Delk	5-9	3-6	0-0	1	0	0	0	13
Anthony Epps	4-7	2-4	1-3	5	4	0	1	11
Jeff Sheppard	2-4	1-2	2-4	4	3	0	2	7
Jared Prickett	0-4	0-1	3-4	9	2	2	1	3
Antoine Walker	6-9	1-2	0-2	3	3	0	2	13
Andre Riddick	2-3	0-0	2-3	6	1	3	4	6
Allen Edwards	0-1	0-1	0-0	0	0	0	1	0
Scott Padgett	1-3	1-3	4-4	2	0	0	1	7
Chris Harrison	2-3	2-3	0-0	2	0	0	1	6
Cameron Mills	0-0	0-0	1-2	0	0	0	1	1
Team rebounds				3				
Totals	**31-60**	**11-25**	**17-27**	**50**	**19**	**10**	**19**	**90**

Boston University	21	28 —	49
Kentucky	50	40 —	90

Turnovers: Boston U. 26, Kentucky 24
Technicals: none
Officials: Tom Lopes, Willy Guardiolia, Phil Robinson
Attendance: 23,650

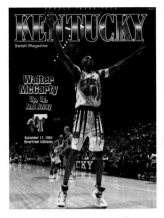

1994

Dec. 17

Riverfront Coliseum • Cincinnati, Ohio

Texas Tech	68
Kentucky	83

"Texas Tech is as tough and as good as any SEC team. It's a very big, very tough basketball team ... Rodrick was outstanding tonight, and Shep did a great job with his one-on-one play."

— Rick Pitino

Before the season began, two NBA scouts warned Rick Pitino that the toughest opponent UK would face in December wouldn't be UCLA or Indiana. That distinction, they predicted, belonged to Texas Tech. And their glimpse into the crystal ball wasn't far off-base, either, because this game, played in a packed-to-the-rafters Riverfront Coliseum in Cincinnati, was much closer than the final score indicates. In fact, the Cats had to overcome an early eight-point (13-5) deficit, and didn't take the lead for good until a pair of Anthony Epps free throws made it 29-28 with 5:20 left in the opening half. Those freebies, which came courtesy of a technical foul on Tech's Mark Davis, may have been the turning point in the game. From there, the Cats went on a 14-5 run to close out the half, then opened the second frame with a 17-7 spurt that gave them a 60-40 lead with 13:40 left to play. Jeff Sheppard and Jared

Prickett came off the bench to provide the firepower for UK's comeback. Sheppard had eight of his 10 points in the opening half, while Prickett had six boards. In the end, however, the game belonged to Rodrick Rhodes, who turned in his finest performance of the young season with 23 points, six rebounds and four assists. After two

Rhodes free throws gave UK its biggest lead, 70-49, with 6:57 left, Tech managed to trim the difference to 10 with just more than two minutes remaining. The Cats were able to hang on for the victory by sinking five free throws — two each by Rhodes and Walter McCarty and one by Epps — while limiting Tech to a single basket.

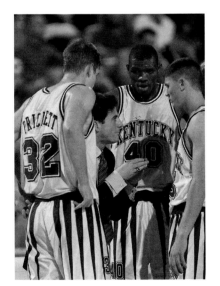

Texas Tech	fg-a	3-pt	ft-a	rb	a	b	pf	tp
Darvin Ham	2-3	0-0	0-0	8	1	0	4	4
Jason Sasser	4-14	0-0	9-11	7	1	0	3	17
Mark Davis	6-19	0-1	1-5	7	6	0	3	13
Koy Smith	2-3	1-2	2-2	2	2	0	2	7
Lance Hughes	6-11	2-5	2-4	5	1	1	3	16
Gionet Cooper	0-2	0-1	1-2	2	0	0	3	1
Jason Martin	4-8	0-1	0-0	0	2	0	3	8
Tony Battie	1-1	0-0	0-0	3	1	0	5	2
Cory Carr	0-1	0-1	0-0	0	0	0	0	0
Team rebounds				3				
Totals	**25-62**	**3-11**	**15-24**	**37**	**14**	**1**	**26**	**68**
Kentucky	fg-a	3-pt	ft-a	rb	a	b	pf	tp
Rodrick Rhodes	5-7	1-1	12-15	6	4	0	2	23
Walter McCarty	3-4	0-1	3-4	5	2	3	4	9
Mark Pope	2-2	0-0	0-1	2	1	1	4	4
Tony Delk	7-12	0-2	0-1	2	3	0	2	14
Anthony Epps	2-8	1-4	5-6	0	4	0	2	10
Andre Riddick	2-5	0-0	0-0	5	0	1	2	4
Jeff Sheppard	5-9	0-0	0-2	3	2	0	1	10
Jared Prickett	2-7	0-0	3-4	8	5	0	4	7
Antoine Walker	1-5	0-0	0-0	2	1	0	1	2
Chris Harrison	0-0	0-0	0-0	0	0	0	0	0
Allen Edwards	0-0	0-0	0-0	0	0	0	0	0
Team rebounds				6				
Totals	**29-59**	**2-8**	**23-33**	**39**	**22**	**5**	**22**	**83**

Texas Tech	33	35	—	68
Kentucky	43	40	—	83

Turnovers: Texas Tech 25, Kentucky 22
Technicals: Texas Tech — Mark Davis; Texas Tech — bench
Officials: Gary Marcum, Mike Thibodeaux, Doug Shows
Attendance: 17,153

Watching a Wildcat practice session is no different than sitting in a classroom. Rick Pitino considers himself a teacher, and when you watch him at work during practice, you understand why. He never stops teaching, often interrupting the action to point out the right or wrong of a particular play, or of a sequence of events, and the reason why he was pleased or displeased. UK practices, which are always closed to the public, are extremely intense, oftentimes more so than the actual games. Even a game day walk-through is serious business. The two areas that are most heavily emphasized are shooting and defense. Each Wildcat player usually practices twice a day. At some point in the morning or early afternoon, the player gets with one of the assistant coaches and spends an hour working on individual skills. Pitino gives great freedom to his assistants, so it's not unusual for one of them to stop the flow of action to make a point.

Because of Pitino's emphasis on preparation, virtually every team practice begins with a 30-45 minute film session. During the on-court practice, there is more four-on-four competition than three-on-three or five-on-five. The players are divided into three four-man teams (blue, white and red) for most drills involving the press, press offense and halfcourt defense. No one sits during a practice. Players not actively involved stand on the sidelines waiting for a chance to replace a teammate. Even injured players, if their injury allows, don't remain idle, usually spending some time on the treadmill. Practices vary in length from three hours during the early part of the season to just over an hour during the final few weeks. Every practice ends with the players gathered around Pitino at mid-court, hands high and saying in unison, "hard work."

PRACTICE

Striving to Improve

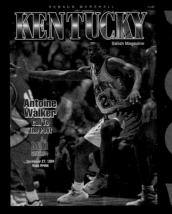

Marshall 75
Kentucky 116

1994 Dec. 27

Rupp Arena • Lexington, Ky.

"It's tougher coaching against Billy than it is against Ralph (Willard) or Tubby (Smith), because Billy has been like a son to me."

— Rick Pitino

"Coming and playing in Rupp Arena was a lot easier the last five years than it was tonight."

— Billy Donovan

Rick Pitino humorously warned fans that "the Marshall Plan" was in effect, but what he didn't say was that there would be an alternate strategy as well — the "Sheppard Plan." With sophomore guard Jeff Sheppard making good on five of six first-half three-point attempts, the Cats raced to a 66-35 lead by the end of the half, then never looked back against an upstart Marshall team coached by Pitino protégé Billy Donovan and former Wildcat John Pelphrey. During one stretch in the opening 20 minutes, UK connected on 13 of 16 shots. Sheppard, who was making his initial start at point guard, had 19 of his 21 points by intermission, including nine of the Cats' first 13. Apparently, Sheppard's long-range accuracy was catching, for by game's end the Cats had connected on 15 of 28 three-point attempts. Kentucky's

defense once again dominated the game, holding the Thundering Herd to below 32 percent shooting from the field while forcing 29 turnovers. The Herd's big gun, Shawn Moore, was held to 13 points on three of 17 shooting. On offense, the Cats were sharp, slick and unselfish, as evidenced by

their 32 assists. Tony Delk (14), Andre Riddick (12), Jared Prickett (12), Antoine Walker (11) and Mark Pope (10) provided strong scoring support for Sheppard. Riddick and Pope pulled down 12 and 10 rebounds, respectively, to help give Kentucky a 49-41 edge in the board war.

Marshall	fg-a	3-pt	ft-a	rb	a	b	pf	tp
Shawn Moore	3-17	1-7	6-8	9	3	1	1	13
Troy Gray	6-12	1-3	7-8	6	0	0	4	20
Curtis Raymond	3-9	0-2	0-0	6	1	1	4	6
Tink Brown	3-5	1-2	5-6	0	3	0	3	12
Doug Schieppe	1-6	0-5	0-0	5	0	0	4	2
Malik Hightower	3-11	1-6	3-4	7	0	0	2	10
Thad Bonapart	3-9	0-0	2-3	3	1	1	3	8
Chris Gray	0-1	0-0	4-4	3	2	0	2	4
Team rebounds				2				
Totals	**22-70**	**4-25**	**27-33**	**41**	**10**	**3**	**23**	**75**

Kentucky	fg-a	3-pt	ft-a	rb	a	b	pf	tp
Rodrick Rhodes	2-8	2-5	2-2	1	5	2	2	8
Walter McCarty	2-4	0-0	4-4	3	4	1	3	8
Andre Riddick	6-9	0-0	0-1	12	2	4	4	12
Tony Delk	5-9	3-7	1-2	2	2	0	2	14
Jeff Sheppard	7-9	5-6	2-2	4	1	1	3	21
Anthony Epps	1-3	0-1	2-2	3	8	0	1	4
Jared Prickett	4-5	0-0	4-5	5	1	2	0	12
Mark Pope	3-7	0-1	4-4	10	1	3	4	10
Antoine Walker	4-8	2-3	1-3	1	6	0	0	11
Chris Harrison	2-3	2-3	0-0	2	1	0	3	6
Allen Edwards	2-7	1-1	3-4	4	0	0	0	8
Scott Padgett	0-3	0-1	0-0	2	1	0	1	0
Cameron Mills	1-1	0-0	0-0	0	0	0	0	2
Team rebounds				1				
Totals	**39-76**	**15-28**	**23-29**	**49**	**32**	**13**	**24**	**116**

Marshall	35	40	— 75
Kentucky	66	50	— 116

Turnovers: Marshall 29, Kentucky 23
Technicals: Kentucky — Antoine Walker; Kentucky — bench
Officials: Gene Monje, David Day, Frank Scagliotta
Attendance: 23,782

Bernard "Peck" Hickman
Head Coach, 1944-67

OFFICIAL GAME PROGRAM $3.00

1995 Jan. 1

Freedom Hall • Louisville, Ky.

Kentucky   86
Louisville   88

"This is a lesson for our team. The team that has more talent doesn't always win. What makes a great team is playing together with great enthusiasm."

— Rick Pitino

"I've never seen him (Wheat) take over a game like that. The game was his. He almost made it look easy."

— Samaki Walker

eJuan Wheat came up big down the stretch and Samaki Walker was a major force in the middle as the Cards notched their first victory over UK since 1989. Wheat's back-to-back three-pointers sparked a crucial drive that saw U of L turn a five-point deficit into a seven-point lead in just more than three minutes. UK, trailing 40-36 at halftime, opened the second half by reeling off eight unanswered points (treys by Tony Delk and Rodrick Rhodes and two free throws by Walter McCarty) to go in front, 44-40. Louisville responded with seven straight points before McCarty's three-pointer knotted the score at 47-47. After a pair of B.J. Flynn freebies gave U of L a 49-47 advantage, Delk, Jared Prickett and Jeff Sheppard accounted for eight points to give UK a 54-49 lead. It was here that things began to unravel for the Cats. Poor shooting from the outside and domination

by Walker in the paint (he had 11 blocked shots) were the Cats' undoing. Over the next three minutes, thanks to eight points from Wheat and four from Alvin Sims, the Cards righted themselves and moved ahead, 63-56. Despite horrendous shooting (34.1 percent), the Cats managed to claw back to within one (82-81) when Tony Delk

hit two free throws and Sheppard knocked in an eight-footer with 56 seconds remaining. After Tick Rogers dropped in two free throws to make it 84-81, Walker snuffed UK's final chance by blocking a Sheppard jumper in the lane. Inside the last 30 seconds, Wheat hit three free throws and Walker one to seal the Cards' victory.

Kentucky	fg-a	3-pt	ft-a	rb	a	b	pf	tp
Rodrick Rhodes	1-9	1-3	2-2	1	0	1	5	5
Walter McCarty	5-11	3-5	4-5	9	1	0	1	17
Andre Riddick	1-3	0-0	0-0	4	1	1	2	2
Tony Delk	9-19	3-8	2-3	8	1	0	3	23
Jeff Sheppard	6-17	2-4	5-6	4	3	1	4	19
Anthony Epps	0-2	0-0	2-2	0	0	0	3	2
Jared Prickett	0-1	0-0	3-4	4	0	0	2	3
Antoine Walker	2-9	0-3	2-2	6	2	0	4	6
Mark Pope	4-10	0-3	1-3	10	1	0	2	9
Allen Edwards	0-1	0-1	0-0	1	1	0	1	0
Chris Harrison	0-0	0-0	0-0	0	0	0	0	0
Team rebounds				5				
Totals	28-82	9-27	21-27	52	10	3	27	86

Louisville	fg-a	3-pt	ft-a	rb	a	b	pf	tp
Eric Johnson	4-8	0-0	0-0	2	0	0	4	8
Jason Osborne	3-7	1-4	5-6	6	2	3	3	12
Samaki Walker	5-8	0-0	4-7	10	1	11	3	14
Tick Rogers	2-9	0-1	7-8	3	2	1	3	11
DeJuan Wheat	7-9	3-4	6-8	4	5	0	1	23
Alvin Sims	2-4	0-0	0-0	5	3	1	2	4
B.J. Flynn	3-9	0-0	3-4	5	2	0	0	9
Beau Zach Smith	2-3	0-0	0-0	0	0	1	3	4
Brian Kiser	1-3	1-2	0-0	2	1	0	3	3
Team rebounds				1				
Totals	29-60	5-11	25-33	38	16	17	22	88

Kentucky	36	50 —	86
Louisville	40	48 —	88

Turnovers: Louisville 17, Kentucky 16
Technicals: none
Officials: Don Rutledge, John Clougherty, Jim Burr
Attendance: 19,841

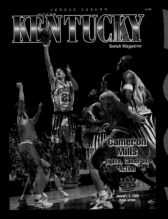

KENTUCKY
Swish Magazine

Cameron Mills
Lights, Cameron, Action

1995
Jan. 4
Rupp Arena • Lexington, Ky.

Auburn	**64**
Kentucky	**98**

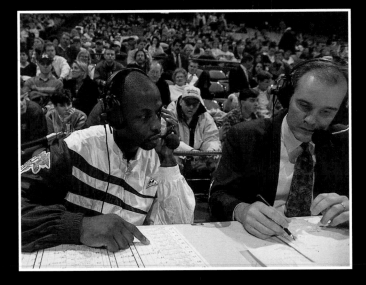

U K bounced back from its disappointing loss at Louisville by turning in one of its best efforts of the campaign against determined-but-outmanned Auburn. Appropriately enough, it was Rodrick Rhodes, whose poor performance against Louisville cost him his starting spot against Auburn, who led the Cats to their impressive victory. Rhodes came off the bench midway through the first half and immediately made his presence felt by hitting a three-pointer. He would finish the night with 23 points in just under 24 minutes of action. UK jumped on top early, grabbing a 7-0 lead on a Jared Prickett free throw, two baskets by Mark Pope and a layup by Walter McCarty. Thanks to Rhodes' 15 first-half points, UK led 45-32 at the half. Early in the second half, it looked like the Tigers might make things interesting when they closed to within 48-41 with 17:16 still left to play. But the chal-

lenge turned out to be little more than fool's gold, and as it had been all season, it was UK's defense that shut down the Auburn threat. While Auburn was stumbling, the Cats were rolling, outscoring their opponents 22-9 over the next few minutes to take a commanding 70-50 lead. The final 34-point margin was

UK's biggest of the night. Rebounding was another big reason why Kentucky was able to come away with such an easy win. UK outrebounded Auburn 51-36, with Pope pulling down 10 for the third consecutive game. Tony Delk broke out of a shooting slump by connecting on eight of 10 attempts.

> "I just wish everyone would focus more on the team and less on me. I get tired of hearing all that Rod Rhodes this and Rod Rhodes that stuff. I just want to be judged like everyone else."
>
> — Rodrick Rhodes

Auburn	fg-a	3-pt	ft-a	rb	a	b	pf	tp
Chris Davis	1-1	0-0	1-4	2	0	0	5	3
Lance Weems	3-8	2-4	0-0	2	1	0	1	8
Moochie Norris	3-7	0-2	0-0	2	2	0	1	6
Pat Burke	7-14	0-0	4-5	11	2	3	2	18
Frank Williams	1-4	0-0	2-4	6	2	0	5	4
Ray Donald	2-6	0-2	3-4	5	3	0	1	7
Jim Costner	4-11	0-0	2-2	2	0	0	3	10
Wes Flanigan	2-4	1-2	3-4	0	1	0	4	8
Leroy Davis	0-1	0-1	0-0	3	0	0	2	0
Team rebounds				3				
Totals	**23-56**	**3-11**	**15-23**	**36**	**11**	**3**	**24**	**64**

Kentucky	fg-a	3-pt	ft-a	rb	a	b	pf	tp
Jared Prickett	3-9	0-0	2-6	8	3	0	3	8
Walter McCarty	5-13	1-4	1-3	7	1	1	3	12
Mark Pope	4-8	0-1	1-2	10	1	2	1	9
Tony Delk	8-10	0-2	2-3	6	4	0	1	18
Jeff Sheppard	1-4	0-2	0-1	1	5	0	1	2
Anthony Epps	1-2	1-2	2-2	3	3	0	1	5
Rodrick Rhodes	6-15	4-10	7-8	3	4	1	4	23
Antoine Walker	5-9	1-3	2-4	5	2	0	2	13
Andre Riddick	1-1	0-0	0-0	2	2	0	2	2
Scott Padgett	1-4	1-3	0-0	1	0	0	1	3
Allen Edwards	1-2	1-1	0-0	0	0	0	1	3
Chris Harrison	0-2	0-1	0-0	2	1	0	0	0
Cameron Mills	0-0	0-0	0-0	1	0	0	1	0
Team rebounds				2				
Totals	**36-79**	**9-29**	**17-29**	**51**	**26**	**4**	**21**	**98**

Auburn	32	32	—	64
Kentucky	45	53	—	98

Turnovers: Auburn 21, Kentucky 9
Technicals: Auburn — Chris Davis
Officials: Don Rutledge, Rusty Herring, Mac Chauvin
Attendance: 23,805

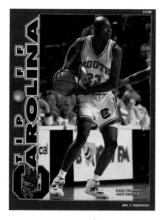

1995 *Jan. 7*

Frank McGuire Arena • Columbia, S.C.

Kentucky	**80**
South Carolina	**55**

"I was waiting for Coach Pitino to come in and hit a three-pointer."

— (USC forward) Malik Russell

UK rode a record-tying three-point performance to its easy win over South Carolina. The Cats riddled South Carolina's zone defense, making good on 17 of 37 three-point attempts. The 17 treys equaled the Southeastern Conference single-game record. In fact, all but 10 of UK's field goals came from behind the three-point arc. During one stretch, 10 straight Wildcat baskets were treys. The Cats were led by a trio of long-range bombers — Tony Delk, Jeff Sheppard and Rodrick Rhodes. Those three accounted for 15 of UK's three-pointers. The Gamecocks, with only eight scholarship players, hung with the Cats until late in the first half, when the three-point shooting barrage began to take its toll. UK's final six buckets of the half were three-pointers, and they were enough to give the Cats a 36-28 lead at the break. The second half was

no contest, thanks to UK's outside gunning and its superiority in numbers. The Cats opened the second half by hitting four quick treys. Delk topped UK in scoring with 18 points, hitting six of 14 three-pointers. All of Delk's field goal attempts were from beyond the three-point stripe. Sheppard had 15 points and Rhodes

added 14. Antoine Walker, Walter McCarty and Anthony Epps each chipped in with seven points. While UK was sizzling from three-point land, the Gamecocks were shooting blanks, missing all 13 trey attempts. UK also whipped South Carolina on the boards, 41-32. Mark Pope and Epps pulled down nine and seven, respectively.

Kentucky	fg-a	3-pt	ft-a	rb	a	b	pf	tp
Rodrick Rhodes	4-8	4-6	2-2	5	4	1	3	14
Antoine Walker	2-5	0-1	3-4	2	3	0	3	7
Mark Pope	1-3	0-0	2-4	9	1	2	2	4
Tony Delk	6-14	6-14	0-0	2	3	0	3	18
Jeff Sheppard	5-12	5-10	0-0	2	3	0	3	15
Jared Prickett	2-4	0-0	0-0	4	1	1	2	4
Walter McCarty	3-6	1-3	0-0	2	1	1	2	7
Andre Riddick	0-0	0-0	0-0	1	0	0	1	0
Allen Edwards	1-1	0-0	0-0	2	0	0	0	2
Anthony Epps	2-4	1-2	2-2	7	3	0	1	7
Scott Padgett	1-2	0-1	0-0	2	0	0	1	2
Team rebounds				3				
Totals	**27-59**	**17-37**	**9-12**	**41**	**19**	**5**	**21**	**80**

South Carolina	fg-a	3-pt	ft-a	rb	a	b	pf	tp
Andy Bostick	3-7	0-3	1-2	6	0	0	4	7
Malik Russell	6-10	0-1	6-6	7	2	2	2	18
Peter Van Elswyk	0-3	0-1	1-2	6	0	0	1	1
Carey Rich	5-13	0-5	2-3	3	2	0	1	12
Melvin Watson	3-9	0-1	4-8	2	3	1	5	10
William Unseld	1-6	0-0	0-0	4	0	0	0	2
George Formanek	0-0	0-0	0-0	0	0	0	1	0
Ryan Stack	2-5	0-2	1-2	1	0	2	0	5
Shawn Wingate	0-1	0-0	0-0	0	0	0	0	0
Team rebounds				3				
Totals	**20-54**	**0-13**	**15-23**	**32**	**7**	**5**	**14**	**55**

Kentucky	36	44	—	80
South Carolina	28	27	—	55

Turnovers: Kentucky 21, South Carolina 16
Technicals: none
Officials: John Clougherty, Kevin Fehr, Leroy Richardson
Attendance: 10,582

1995

Jan. 10

O'Connell Center • Gainesville, Fla.

FLORIDA

Kentucky	83
Florida	67

"This was just one of those nights where we did things like we're supposed to. We played together as a team, we went inside-outside on offense and we got in their face on defense. I only wish we could play like this all the time."

— Rodrick Rhodes

"I don't know what to brag on more, offense or defense. This was one of the better performances we've had at Kentucky."

— Rick Pitino

Near-perfect, dominant, superb, outstanding ... the list of adjectives that describe the Cats' victory over Florida in Gainesville is indeed a long one. In every phase of the game, from start to finish, UK gave a textbook performance on both ends of the court. On offense, UK riddled the 15th-ranked Gators' defense, hitting 57.1 percent from the field. Defensively, UK held the Gators to just 18 field goals on 52 attempts for 34.6 percent. Not surprisingly, the game was never as close as the final score indicates, with UK once owning a 28-point lead (67-39). The Cats wasted no time smothering the Gators, taking a 6-0 lead on consecutive three-pointers by Rodrick Rhodes and Mark Pope. Florida, unable to negotiate successfully against UK's defense, never seriously challenged the Cats. Midway through the half, following a three-point play by Antoine Walker, UK's lead had bal-

looned to 28-14. The Cats, who shot 72.2 percent from the field, led 41-29 at the half, and that lead would have been even bigger had they done better than four for 11 at the free throw line. Florida's hopes of mounting a comeback were quickly quashed when UK went on a

14-3 run to start the second half. UK continued to increase its lead until a three-pointer by Jared Prickett — his first of the season — made it 67-39 with 13:27 left to play. Rhodes, who gave another terrific performance, and Delk led UK in scoring with 17 points each.

Kentucky	fg-a	3-pt	ft-a	rb	a	b	pf	tp
Rodrick Rhodes	6-8	1-1	4-7	4	1	1	3	17
Jared Prickett	4-6	1-1	0-0	1	5	0	2	9
Mark Pope	3-6	1-1	2-4	7	0	1	4	9
Jeff Sheppard	5-8	1-2	0-0	1	3	0	5	11
Tony Delk	6-10	3-5	2-2	7	3	1	3	17
Walter McCarty	2-5	0-2	0-0	6	2	1	3	4
Anthony Epps	0-0	0-0	0-0	1	1	0	1	0
Antoine Walker	5-9	0-1	3-3	3	2	0	3	13
Andre Riddick	0-2	0-0	0-1	1	0	0	1	0
Allen Edwards	1-1	0-0	0-0	0	0	0	0	2
Scott Padgett	0-1	0-1	1-2	1	0	0	0	1
Team rebounds				1				
Totals	32-56	7-14	12-19	33	17	4	25	83

Florida	fg-a	3-pt	ft-a	rb	a	b	pf	tp
Tony Mickens	2-7	0-1	0-0	4	0	0	2	4
Andrew DeClercq	1-4	0-1	7-10	6	2	1	4	9
Dametri Hill	4-10	0-2	2-2	6	1	2	1	10
Greg Williams	2-6	1-2	4-6	2	2	1	1	9
Dan Cross	4-11	2-5	11-12	1	0	0	4	21
Jason Anderson	1-4	0-0	0-0	2	0	0	0	2
Svein Dyrkolbotn	1-1	0-0	0-0	1	0	0	1	2
Dan Williams	1-4	0-1	0-0	1	3	0	0	2
LeRon Williams	1-1	0-0	1-2	1	0	0	2	3
Brian Thompson	1-4	0-0	2-4	3	0	0	1	4
John Griffiths	0-0	0-0	0-0	0	0	1	2	0
Damon Maddox	0-0	0-0	1-2	0	0	0	0	1
Clayton Bates	0-0	0-0	0-0	0	0	0	0	0
Team rebounds				8				
Totals	18-52	3-12	28-38	35	8	5	18	67

Kentucky	41	42	—	83
Florida	29	38	—	67

Turnovers: Kentucky 16, Florida 15
Technicals: none
Officials: Leroy Richardson, Tom O'Neill, Gary Marcum
Attendance: 11,902

KENTUCKY
Swish Magazine

Anthony Epps
Making
His Point

January 14, 1995
Rupp Arena

1995

Jan. 14

Rupp Arena • Lexington, Ky.

Georgia 71
Kentucky 83

"I'm happy we won. I'm very unhappy with the way we played today. There's not much good I can say. We did not block out and rebound the basketball. We did not grab the basketball. We did not execute. All the great things we saw in the Florida game were not present."

— Rick Pitino

"I feel like we lost. But we won. Let's talk about winning the game."

— Rodrick Rhodes

I f the adjective artistic comes to mind when describing the Cats' win at Florida, then nightmarish is the term that jumps out at you when describing this victory. So bad were the Cats that Rick Pitino ordered his players back into the gym for a midnight practice only hours after the game had finished. What bothered Pitino? What didn't? Execution, rebounding, defense, handling the ball, lead management ... those were but a few of the areas that Pitino later signaled out as trouble spots. Despite the poor performance, the Cats were able to handle a big, physical and talented Georgia club, and they did it with relative ease. The main reason was Georgia's inability to hit the bucket, especially in the first half. During those 20 minutes, the Dawgs made just six baskets in 25 attempts. The result was a 38-24 UK lead. The Cats got a strong boost in the opening half from subs Antoine Walker, Anthony Epps and Scott Padgett. Walker had four points and six rebounds, Epps had four points and two assists, while Padgett knocked in five points in just two minutes of playing time. Unfortunately, none of the Cats were able to rise above the muck of the second half. UK built a 21-point cushion with nine minutes left, then allowed it to be chopped to nine with 1:36 remaining. Five missed free throws by UK let the Dawgs have a second life and make things mildly interesting. But when guard Pertha Robinson lost the ball out of bounds while driving to the basket, the Georgia threat was ended.

Georgia	fg-a	3-pt	ft-a	rb	a	b	pf	tp
Ty Wilson	0-8	0-6	0-0	2	2	0	1	0
Steve Jones	1-2	0-0	2-4	5	1	1	0	4
Pertha Robinson	2-7	0-2	7-8	5	6	0	4	11
Katu Davis	7-13	0-4	4-5	5	1	0	2	18
Carlos Strong	2-6	0-0	2-2	6	0	1	2	6
Charles Claxton	3-6	0-1	5-8	5	0	3	4	11
Curtis Carrington	1-4	0-2	4-4	5	0	0	1	6
Shandon Anderson	5-10	0-0	1-2	2	1	0	5	11
Terrell Bell	1-2	0-1	2-6	1	1	0	3	4
Team rebounds				6				
Totals	22-58	0-16	27-39	42	12	5	22	71

Kentucky	fg-a	3-pt	ft-a	rb	a	b	pf	tp
Tony Delk	8-15	1-4	0-2	4	2	0	4	17
Andre Riddick	2-2	0-0	1-2	4	0	0	4	5
Rodrick Rhodes	3-7	1-2	4-4	3	3	0	4	11
Jeff Sheppard	3-7	0-2	1-2	0	0	2	1	7
Allen Edwards	0-1	0-0	0-0	0	2	0	1	0
Antoine Walker	3-7	1-2	1-2	7	2	0	2	8
Anthony Epps	3-6	0-0	2-2	3	7	0	1	8
Jared Prickett	3-9	1-2	0-1	10	0	1	3	7
Scott Padgett	1-2	1-1	2-2	0	0	0	0	5
Walter McCarty	2-6	0-1	0-0	3	1	1	3	4
Mark Pope	2-6	1-3	3-6	4	3	0	3	8
Chris Harrison	1-3	1-2	0-0	0	0	0	2	3
Team rebounds				7				
Totals	31-71	7-19	14-23	45	20	4	28	83

Georgia	24	47	—	71
Kentucky	38	45	—	83

Turnovers: Georgia 25, Kentucky 20
Technicals: none
Officials: Don Rutledge, Tom Eades, Gary Marcum
Attendance: 23,625

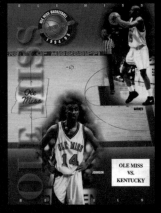

1995

Jan. 18

The Pyramid • Memphis, Tenn.

OLE MISS
VS.
KENTUCKY

Kentucky 82
Ole Miss 65

"We knew we had to keep coming at them, that we couldn't let up. Coach told us that if we didn't match their intensity, then we wouldn't win. I guess we matched it."

— Anthony Epps

"Kentucky has a lot of weapons. They kept bringing them at us. They are huge, and they are talented. We just ran out of gas."

— (Ole Miss coach) Rob Evans

For the second straight outing, the Cats won despite turning in a performance that was something less than an artistic masterpiece. Cold shooting from the field, (41.1 percent overall, three of 16 from beyond the three-point arc) kept the Cats in hot water until late in the game when they were finally able to pull away from the upset-minded Rebels. Much of UK's shooting woes could be attributed to the Rebels' good defense and to their willingness to foul rather than give up easy shots. In all, the Cats shot 42 free throws, making 33. The biggest benefactor of the Rebs' fouling was Rodrick Rhodes. The 6-6 junior, who finished with a game-best 23 points, made good on 16 of 20 attempts. The Cats' poor shooting was in stark contrast to the last time they played in The Pyramid, when they blistered the nets en route to winning the 1994 SEC Tournament. In that tourney, the three-point shot was a decisive weapon; against the Rebels, however, it was mostly missing in action. UK missed its first 13 three-point attempts, and didn't make one until Anthony Epps connected with 3:46 remaining. So cold were the Cats that they managed just a single bucket during the final 12 minutes of the first half, which ended with the Rebels leading 34-33. Unable to connect from the outside, UK started pounding the ball down low, and that's when Ole Miss began fouling. Free throws, it turned out, proved to be UK's savior. Tony Delk had 18 points for the Cats, while Epps and Andre Riddick each had 12. Riddick, who got the start at center, also had nine rebounds and four blocked shots.

Kentucky	fg-a	3-pt	ft-a	rb	a	b	pf	tp
Walter McCarty	3-5	0-1	2-3	2	1	1	1	8
Rodrick Rhodes	3-9	1-1	16-20	5	3	0	1	23
Andre Riddick	4-5	0-0	4-6	9	0	4	5	12
Jeff Sheppard	1-4	0-1	2-2	5	5	0	4	4
Tony Delk	7-19	1-7	3-3	4	0	0	3	18
Antoine Walker	1-3	0-1	1-2	4	0	0	2	3
Anthony Epps	3-8	1-4	5-6	1	2	0	0	12
Jared Prickett	1-1	0-0	0-0	1	1	0	4	2
Mark Pope	0-2	0-1	0-0	3	1	1	4	0
Team rebounds				1				
Totals	**23-56**	**3-16**	**33-42**	**35**	**13**	**6**	**24**	**82**

Ole Miss	fg-a	3-pt	ft-a	rb	a	b	pf	tp
Anthony Boone	5-12	0-0	5-8	8	2	1	1	15
Fred Johnigan	2-5	0-2	1-2	2	1	0	3	5
John Jackson	2-7	0-0	7-8	7	3	1	1	11
David Johnson	4-14	0-0	3-6	2	1	1	5	11
Cedric Brim	2-6	1-5	0-0	4	5	0	4	5
Ansu Sesay	4-8	2-5	0-0	8	2	2	4	10
Robert Butler	1-9	0-6	1-2	5	0	0	4	3
L.J. Goolsby	0-0	0-0	0-0	1	0	0	2	0
J.J. Sims	2-2	0-0	1-2	5	0	1	4	5
Team rebounds				6				
Totals	**22-63**	**3-18**	**18-28**	**48**	**14**	**6**	**28**	**65**

Kentucky	33	49 —	82
Ole Miss	34	31 —	65

Turnovers: Ole Miss 24, Kentucky 14
Technicals: Ole Miss — Rob Evans (head coach)
Officials: John Clougherty, David Day, Curtis Shaw
Attendance: 12,073

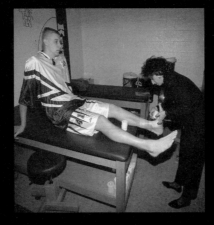

Time spent on the basketball court, either for practice or for games, represents but a small fraction of a UK player's day. Attending classes, watching tape on opponents, working out in the weight room, getting treatment for injuries and studying in the CATS academic center keep the Kentucky players on the go for much of the day. On those rare occasions when they do find some spare time on their hands, they can usually be found hanging out together, listening to music or catching a game on television. The two most private sanctuaries for the players are the Wildcat Lodge and the lounge in Memorial Coliseum. UK's facilities are first-rate, from the state-of-the-art weight room to the hugely successful CATS center. Behind the scenes is also where you can find five of the most important people involved with UK basketball — CATS supervisor Bob Bradley, strength coach Shaun Brown,

trainer JoAnn Hauser, team physician Dr. David Caborn and equipment manager Bill Keightley. All five have enormous responsibilities. It's up to Brown to get the players in shape, then devise a separate plan for each individual Wildcat to follow as the season progresses. Hauser treats everything from a sprained ankle to a pulled muscle to a broken nose. During the course of a season, Hauser estimates that she uses in excess of 1,500 rolls of tape. Caborn handles the more serious injuries, most notably those requiring surgery. Bradley makes sure the players stay on top of their studies. However, it's Keightley, the legendary Mr. Wildcat, who is the heart and soul of the UK program. His duties are endless, ranging from getting the players dressed for practice or a game to offering a hug and a bit of encouragement to a struggling player. The UK players are indeed lucky to have these five in their corner.

WILDCATS

On Campus with the

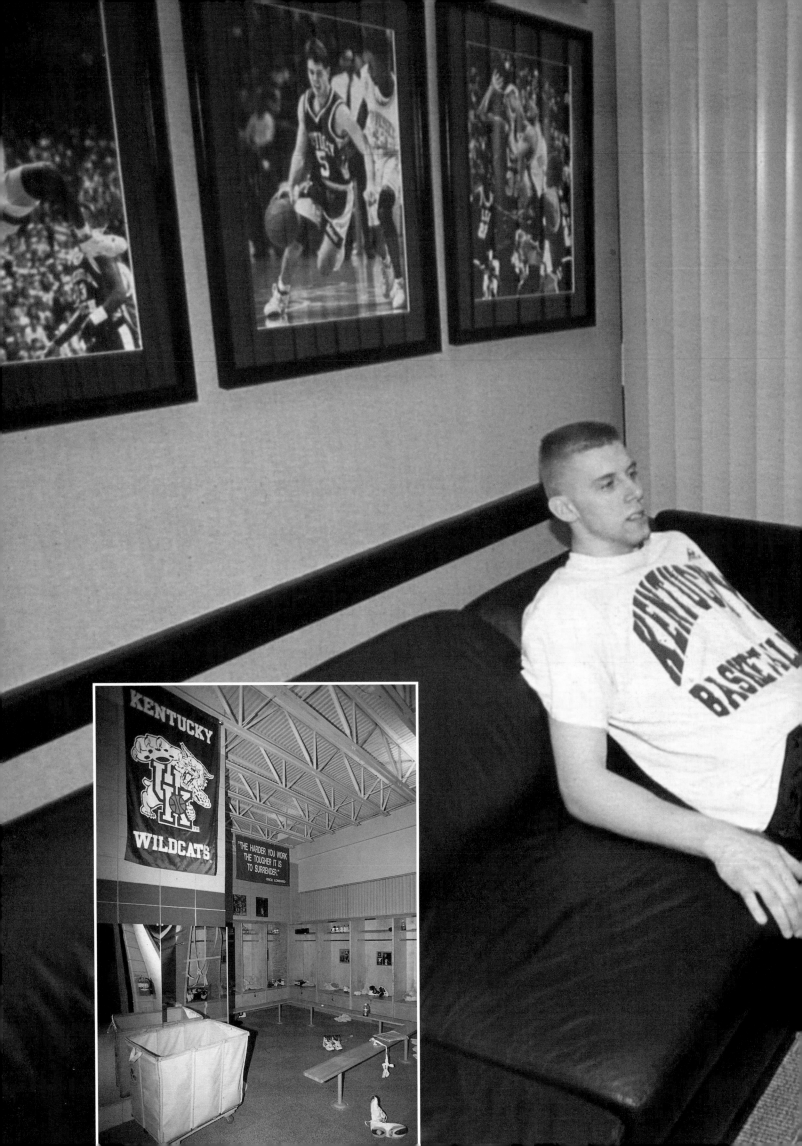

KENTUCKY WILDCATS

"THE HARDER YOU WORK THE TOUGHER IT IS TO SURRENDER." VINCE LOMBARDI

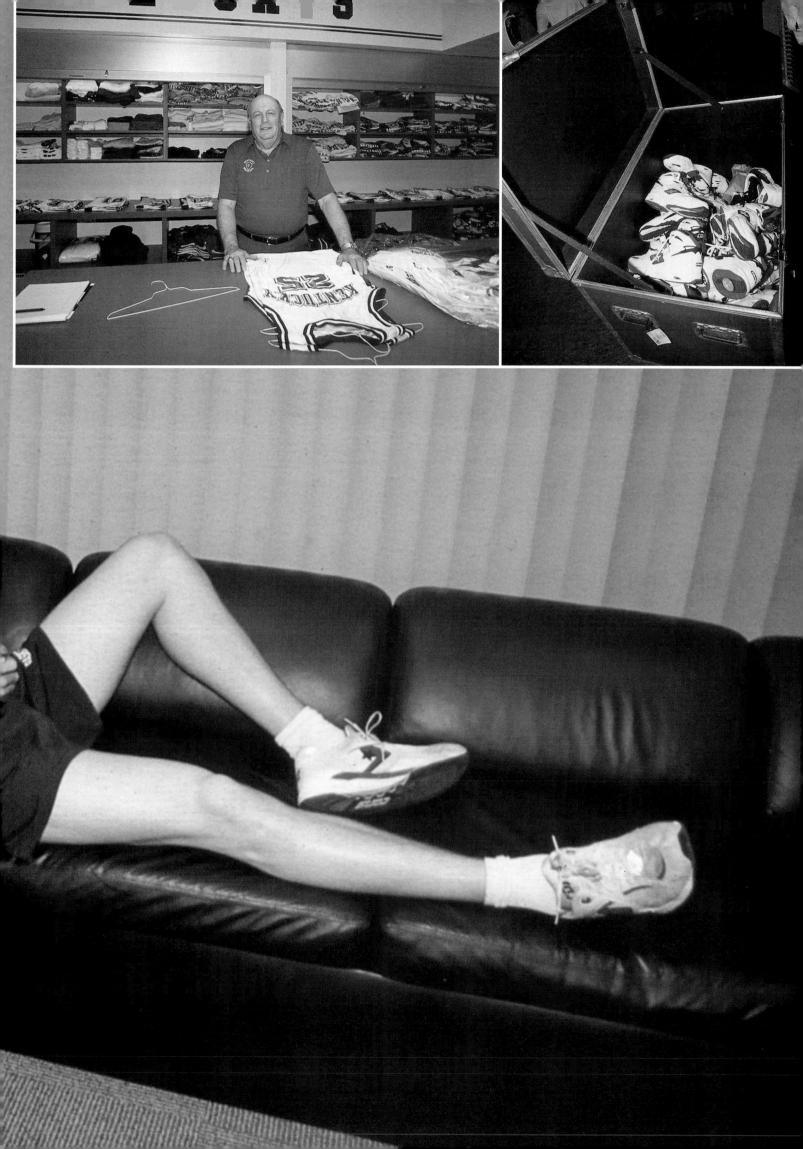

**Game day in Lexington:
The Civic Center**

December 7, 1994
Indiana vs. Kentucky

Vanderbilt 68
Kentucky 81

"When he (McCarty) left the floor, I didn't think he'd get there. I definitely thought it'd be a back-rim job and go out 20 feet."

— Rick Pitino

Just when it looked as if the Commodores were about to pull off a huge upset, a 20-0 run by UK, punctuated by Walter McCarty's highlight-film slam dunk, was more than enough to turn the tide in the Cats' favor and give them the 1,600th victory in the school's storied basketball history. McCarty's thunderous dunk over Vandy's startled J.J. Lucas came with just under three minutes remaining. When McCarty's long flight ended, the Cats were leading 77-59. Only four minutes earlier, things weren't looking so cozy for UK, which had watched Vanderbilt overcome a six-point halftime deficit to take a 59-57 lead. It was at this point, however, that the Commodores' ship began to sink. For the next 14 possessions, covering almost eight minutes, Vanderbilt could do nothing but shoot blanks. The Cats, meanwhile, were hammering the visitors with textbook stuff on both ends of the court. A twisting, acro-

batic layup by Andre Riddick that made it 62-59 seemed to ignite both the UK team and the Rupp Arena crowd. So did the UK defense, which turned the once-confident Commodores into a stumbling, bumbling club that could seemingly do nothing right. Between Riddick's layup and McCarty's jam, a game that looked to be a down-to-

the-wire thriller dissolved into a one-sided romp for UK. Tony Delk, who did not make his first basket until the 5:40 mark of the opening half, connected on six three-pointers and led UK with 24 points. Vandy's veteran guard Ronnie McMahan led his team with 19 points. The loss was the Commodores' 22nd straight in Rupp Arena.

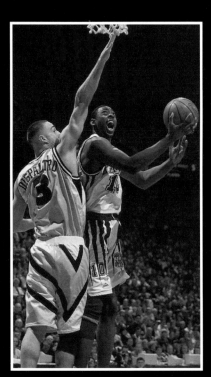

Vanderbilt	fg-a	3-pt	ft-a	rb	a	b	pf	tp
J.J. Lucas	5-12	0-1	0-0	7	1	2	3	10
Frank Seckar	1-4	1-4	0-1	4	2	0	2	3
Ronnie McMahan	6-14	4-8	3-4	5	1	1	2	19
Bryan Milburn	1-5	0-0	2-2	4	1	1	5	4
Drew Maddux	3-11	2-4	3-3	6	2	0	3	11
Malik Evans	3-5	1-1	4-5	7	2	1	4	11
Chris Woods	0-1	0-0	2-2	4	0	5	1	2
Howard Pride	1-6	0-3	2-2	3	3	0	1	4
Pax Whitehead	0-2	0-1	0-0	1	0	0	0	0
Billy DiSpaltro	2-3	0-0	0-2	3	0	0	1	4
Team rebounds				4				
Totals	22-63	8-22	16-21	48	12	10	22	68

Kentucky	fg-a	3-pt	ft-a	rb	a	b	pf	tp
Rodrick Rhodes	2-6	0-1	0-0	1	2	0	2	4
Antoine Walker	2-6	0-0	0-1	5	0	0	1	4
Andre Riddick	4-11	0-0	0-1	8	1	2	4	8
Tony Delk	8-16	6-9	2-4	4	0	1	2	24
Jeff Sheppard	1-5	0-2	1-2	2	3	1	2	3
Anthony Epps	1-4	1-3	4-8	4	6	0	2	7
Walter McCarty	2-5	0-1	2-4	8	2	1	4	6
Mark Pope	4-11	1-2	0-0	9	2	1	1	9
Jared Prickett	7-9	0-0	2-4	3	3	0	0	16
Allen Edwards	0-1	0-0	0-0	1	0	0	1	0
Team rebounds				4				
Totals	31-74	8-18	11-24	49	19	6	19	81

Vanderbilt	35	33 —	68
Kentucky	41	40 —	81

Turnovers: Vanderbilt 17, Kentucky 10
Technicals: none
Officials: Gerald Boudreaux, Joe Mingle, Kevin Fehr
Attendance: 23,222

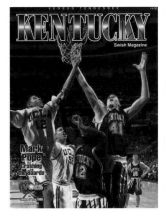

Tennessee 50
Kentucky 69

1995

Jan. 25

Rupp Arena • Lexington, Ky.

"It's a great honor to reach this goal, but for a while, I was wondering if I was going to do it tonight. I mean, I missed a lot of shots. I could hear Coach Pitino from the bench saying, 'He needs a three. Set him up.' Then everything got tight. My arm got tight. The rim got smaller."

— Rodrick Rhodes

Rodrick Rhodes turned a night of personal glory into a night of misery for the visiting Volunteers and their first-year coach Kevin O'Neill. Rhodes, the 6-6 junior from Jersey City, N.J., scored a career-high 29 points for UK, and in so doing became just the 41st Wildcat player to reach the 1,000-point milestone. He reached that celebrated goal when he swished a three-pointer with 49.9 seconds left to play. The Cats needed Rhodes' explosion to put away a Tennessee team bent on using a patient and deliberate offense to overcome its extreme physical and talent shortcomings. That strategy worked early, and the Cats, caught in the slow-down funk, struggled to a 16-14 lead midway through the first half. A late 12-3 run enabled the Cats to up their lead to 28-17 at the half. Thanks to Rhodes and a devastating defense, the second half was all UK. After the Vols chopped a 32-17 UK

lead to 32-23, the Cats went on a 12-0 run that broke the game open. Antoine Walker started the explosion by scoring four straight points. Jeff Sheppard and Mark Pope followed with a three-pointer each, before Sheppard came up with a steal and dunk that made it 44-23. From that point on, the only remaining drama was whether Rhodes

would join UK's select 1,000-point club. UK's defense once again stood out, holding Tennessee to 29.4 percent field goal shooting while causing 27 turnovers. In addition, the Cats came up with 16 steals. Sheppard and Tony Delk had 12 and 11 points, respectively, for UK. Steve Hamer topped the Vols with 18 points.

Tennessee	fg-a	3-pt	ft-a	rb	a	b	pf	tp
Damon Johnson	3-12	0-2	2-2	7	6	0	3	8
Shane Carnes	3-8	2-6	0-0	4	2	0	4	8
Steve Hamer	4-10	0-0	10-11	11	0	3	2	18
Alico Dunk	0-3	0-0	0-0	3	1	0	1	0
Shane Williams	3-6	2-5	2-2	3	1	0	4	10
Kevin Whitted	2-12	0-0	2-2	5	0	2	5	6
Jason Moore	0-0	0-0	0-0	0	0	0	0	0
Team rebounds				6				
Totals	**15-51**	**4-13**	**16-17**	**39**	**10**	**5**	**19**	**50**

Kentucky	fg-a	3-pt	ft-a	rb	a	b	pf	tp
Rodrick Rhodes	11-27	5-13	2-4	2	2	0	2	29
Walter McCarty	0-3	0-2	0-0	2	1	1	4	0
Andre Riddick	1-3	0-0	2-4	6	0	1	5	4
Tony Delk	3-11	1-4	4-4	5	2	2	0	11
Jeff Sheppard	4-7	1-4	3-4	4	5	1	2	12
Anthony Epps	1-2	1-2	0-0	1	2	0	0	3
Antoine Walker	2-4	0-1	0-1	7	1	0	0	4
Mark Pope	1-5	1-3	0-0	6	1	0	3	3
Jared Prickett	0-2	0-0	1-2	4	0	0	1	1
Allen Edwards	0-0	0-0	0-0	0	1	0	0	0
Scott Padgett	0-0	0-0	1-2	0	0	0	0	1
Chris Harrison	0-0	0-0	1-2	0	0	0	1	1
Team rebounds				3				
Totals	**23-64**	**9-29**	**14-23**	**40**	**15**	**5**	**18**	**69**

Tennessee	17	33	—	50
Kentucky	28	41	—	69

Turnovers: Tennessee 27, Kentucky 14
Technicals: none
Officials: Don Rutledge, Tom O'Neill, Bennie Adams
Attendance: 23,427

RAZORBACK
GAMEDAY

1995

Jan. 29

Bud Walton Arena • Fayetteville, Ark.

$2

The Kentucky Game

Kentucky 92
Arkansas 94

"We don't like to lose, but I definitely think it'll make us a better team. I think it was one of the better games we played this season. We couldn't play any better than that."

— Rick Pitino

"Delk really never hurt us before. But Tony had a phenomenal basketball game today."

— (Arkansas coach)
Nolan Richardson

cotty Thurman's three-pointer with 11 seconds left to play lifted Arkansas to a thrilling victory over UK in what may arguably have been the finest college basketball game of the 1994-95 season. Thurman's bucket put the Hogs in front 93-92, and after Jeff Sheppard was stripped of the ball while attempting a shot, Clint McDaniel sank one of two free throws to account for the final margin. From the opening tip-off to the final buzzer, the game was played at a championship level by players on both clubs who continually rose to heroic heights. No one came up bigger than Tony Delk, whose 17 first half points had the Cats poised to take a lead into the dressing room at intermission, only to see that lead disappear when the Hogs' Reggie Garrett hit a 44-footer from midcourt at the horn. Arkansas overcame a nine-point UK lead during a first half that saw the red-hot

Delk connect on four of six three-point attempts. In the second half, it was UK's turn to show its character by erasing an eight-point (76-68) deficit midway through the half. Again, it was Delk who fueled the comeback charge, scoring eight quick points to close the gap to 78-76. Following a pair of Corliss

Williamson free throws that made it 80-76, two freebies by Anthony Epps and a basket each by Delk and Walter McCarty gave UK an 82-80 lead with 5:19 left. Arkansas, sparked by two Williamson free throws, a three-point play by Corey Beck and a trey by Thurman, roared back on top 88-84 at the four-minute

Kentucky	fg-a	3-pt	ft-a	rb	a	b	pf	tp
Rodrick Rhodes	4-13	1-6	2-2	3	7	0	2	11
Walter McCarty	7-9	2-3	0-0	7	2	0	4	16
Andre Riddick	1-6	0-0	0-1	8	1	3	4	2
Tony Delk	9-15	6-9	7-8	3	2	0	3	31
Jeff Sheppard	5-9	2-5	2-2	3	2	0	5	14
Jared Prickett	1-2	0-0	0-0	1	0	0	2	2
Anthony Epps	2-3	2-3	2-2	0	4	0	0	8
Antoine Walker	1-3	1-1	0-0	1	1	1	1	3
Mark Pope	1-2	0-0	3-4	2	0	0	4	5
Chris Harrison	0-1	0-1	0-0	0	0	0	1	0
Scott Padgett	0-0	0-0	0-0	0	0	0	0	0
Allen Edwards	0-1	0-1	0-0	0	0	0	0	0
Team rebounds				4				
Totals	31-64	14-29	16-19	32	19	4	26	92

Arkansas	fg-a	3-pt	ft-a	rb	a	b	pf	tp
Corliss Williamson	9-15	0-0	10-13	9	3	3	1	28
Scotty Thurman	5-6	4-5	8-8	4	2	0	2	22
Dwight Stewart	2-7	2-5	0-0	3	2	2	5	6
Clint McDaniel	2-5	1-4	4-6	1	4	0	2	9
Corey Beck	2-5	0-1	4-5	6	8	0	4	8
Reggie Garrett	3-6	1-2	1-1	0	0	0	4	8
Darnell Robinson	4-8	0-2	0-0	4	1	1	1	8
Alex Dillard	2-4	1-2	0-0	0	0	0	1	5
Lee Wilson	0-1	0-0	0-0	2	0	1	0	0
Landis Williams	0-0	0-0	0-0	0	0	0	0	0
Team rebounds				4				
Totals	29-57	9-21	27-33	33	20	7	20	94

Kentucky	47	49	—	92
Arkansas	49	45	—	94

Turnovers: Arkansas 18, Kentucky 15
Technicals: Kentucky — Jeff Sheppard
Officials: John Clougherty, Tom Lopes, David Day
Attendance: 20,298

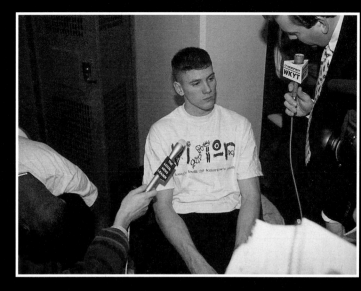

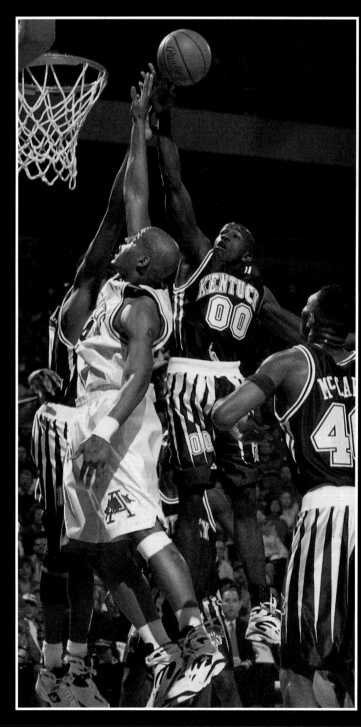

mark. A Mark Pope layup, followed by a Sheppard 14-footer knotted the count at 88-88. Two free throws by Thurman were countered by a Rodrick Rhodes 10-footer, making it 90-90. After McDaniel made good on one of two free tosses, McCarty gave UK its final lead by scoring on a follow-up with 24 seconds remaining. With the game on the line, the Hogs went to their Mr. Clutch, Thurman, whose three-pointer beat Duke in the 1994 NCAA championship game. After using his left arm to nudge defender Sheppard out of the way, Thurman launched what proved to be the game-winner from 18 feet away. Sheppard then raced up court, looking to take a shot over Beck, only to have McDaniel strip him of the ball with less than a second left. Sheppard fouled McDaniel, who made the first free throw, then missed the second. Pope was able to launch a court-length shot

that landed short as the buzzer sounded. Both teams shot well — Arkansas hitting 50.9 percent, UK 48.4 percent — with the Cats being extremely hot from three-point range (14 of 29). Delk led all scorers with a career-high 31 points despite not scoring in the game's final 6:53. McCarty chipped in with 16 points, while Sheppard added 14. The Hogs were led by their potent one-two punch of Williamson and Thurman, who had 28 and 22 points, respectively.

"Probably the greatest
college basketball
game that's probably
been played
in history."

— (Arkansas coach)

Nolan Richardson

A Day in the Life of

Tony Delk

(March 1, 1995)

9 a.m. — Wake up.

9:30 a.m. — Have breakfast in Wildcat Lodge. Turkey-bacon sandwich, Frosted Flakes, milk.

10:30 a.m. — Practice at Memorial Coliseum. Coach Pitino and Coach Brooks were away on a recruiting trip, so Coach O'Brien and Coach Bennett conducted practice. Coach O'Brien really stressed mental toughness, then told us that we'd worked too hard and been through too much to let Georgia beat us.

11:45 a.m. — Bus transports team to Blue Grass Airport.

12:30 p.m. — Charter plane departs.

1:35 p.m. — Arrive in Athens. Bus takes team to Ramada Inn. Andre and I are in the same room. We get a couple of hours sleep.

4:30 p.m. — Pre-game meal at hotel. Fillet, chicken, mashed potatoes, pasta, green beans, carrots, waffles and fruit served.

4:45 p.m. — Watch film of Georgia and finalize game plan. Stopping Georgia in transition and not giving up the three are the main points that Coach Pitino emphasized to us.

6:45 p.m. — Leave for Georgia Coliseum.

8 p.m. — UK vs. Georgia. Before the game, I really didn't think too much about what was at stake. I don't think any of us did. We knew our own destiny was in our hands. People had been talking about Mississippi State, about what might or might not happen, but we didn't. We knew that all we had to do was win out and the championship was ours.

10:30 p.m. — Shower, get dressed and meet with the media.

11 p.m. — Bus takes team to airport.

11:30 p.m. — Plane leaves for Lexington. We a have snack on the plane. Hamburgers, chicken sandwiches and soft drinks.

12:40 p.m. — Arrive at Blue Grass Airport.

1 a.m. — Bus transports team to Wildcat Lodge.

1:30 a.m. — I hit the sack.

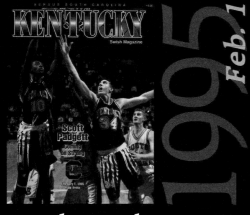

KENTUCKY
Swish Magazine

1995 Feb. 1 *Rupp Arena • Lexington, Ky.*

South Carolina	72
Kentucky	90

"We played good but we didn't play great ... They did the best job of anybody all season against our defense. They play like their last meal is on the table. That's tough to do. It's a credit to them to play that hard and play that well."

— Rick Pitino

"You don't dream. Either you do or you don't. With them (UK), they hit a three, get a steal, make another three and you're out of the game."

— (USC coach) Eddie Fogler

At no time this season were the Cats in a more vulnerable, poised-to-be-bushwhacked position than in their second meeting against South Carolina, a game that was sandwiched between the war at Arkansas and the upcoming struggle against highly ranked Syracuse. And if that wasn't enough of a mine field, the Cats had to play the second half without leading scorer Tony Delk, who injured his shoulder late in the first half. But the upset never materialized. In the end the Cats used their superior size, depth and talent to overwhelm Eddie Fogler's club. UK's inside strength was most evident in the numbers posted by pivot men Andre Riddick and Mark Pope. That duo combined for 25 points, 12 rebounds and two blocked shots. Riddick, in particular, was dominant, and had it not been for early foul troubles he might have enjoyed a

career night. His dozen points came in just 12 minutes of action. Despite UK's clear superiority, the Gamecocks stayed close for much of the first half, pulling to within 31-29 with five minutes left. But a reverse layup by Jared Prickett sparked a 6-0 run that helped UK build a 40-32 lead by halftime. In

the second half, with Delk on the bench, it was Rodrick Rhodes who took charge, scoring 14 of his 19 points after the break. Behind Rhodes' bombing and some nifty passing by Anthony Epps, the Cats were able to steadily pull away for the easy win. Epps handed out 12 assists, while committing only one turnover.

South Carolina	fg-a	3-pt	ft-a	rb	a	b	pf	tp
Carey Rich	5-10	1-4	3-4	3	0	0	2	14
Melvin Watson	5-10	0-3	0-0	2	6	0	3	10
Andy Bostick	2-6	0-2	0-0	3	1	0	1	4
Malik Russell	7-11	2-3	6-11	10	1	1	1	22
Pete Van Elswyk	3-4	0-0	0-1	5	0	0	1	6
William Unseld	2-12	0-1	4-4	6	1	0	1	8
Ryan Stack	2-5	0-1	3-4	2	2	1	4	7
George Formanek	0-1	0-0	1-2	1	0	0	1	1
Shawn Wingate	0-0	0-0	0-0	0	0	0	0	0
Team rebounds				4				
Totals	26-59	3-14	17-26	36	11	2	14	72

Kentucky	fg-a	3-pt	ft-a	rb	a	b	pf	tp
Rodrick Rhodes	7-15	3-7	2-4	5	6	0	4	19
Walter McCarty	4-8	0-1	0-1	5	3	2	1	8
Andre Riddick	6-7	0-0	0-0	5	1	1	5	12
Tony Delk	3-6	2-3	1-2	1	0	0	0	9
Jeff Sheppard	4-10	1-5	2-3	3	0	0	2	11
Anthony Epps	2-8	2-7	2-2	2	12	0	0	8
Mark Pope	4-6	1-2	4-4	7	0	1	3	13
Antoine Walker	3-6	0-0	2-2	6	2	0	1	8
Jared Prickett	1-2	0-0	0-0	1	0	0	1	2
Allen Edwards	0-1	0-1	0-0	0	0	0	2	0
Team rebounds				2				
Totals	34-69	9-26	13-18	37	24	4	19	90

South Carolina	32	40	—	72
Kentucky	40	50	—	90

Turnovers: South Carolina 20, Kentucky 13
Technicals: none
Officials: Don Rutledge, Frank Scagliotta, Leroy Richardson
Attendance: 22,740

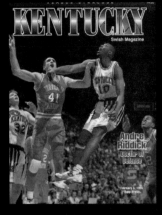

KENTUCKY
Swish Magazine

Andre Riddick
Doctor of Defense

1995

Feb. 5

Rupp Arena • Lexington, Ky.

Syracuse	**71**
Kentucky	**77**

"I don't quite know how to describe this game in words. It was probably their worst performance of the year, and it was probably our worst performance of the year. I think both of us would like to burn the tape and forget about it."

— Rick Pitino

"I don't think the pain in my shoulder affected my shooting that much. Mainly, I just wasn't hitting. The shots were there, but they wouldn't go down."

— Tony Delk

Tony Delk, not even listed as a pre-game starter, shook off the effects of his injured shoulder to score 16 points and lead the Cats to a nationally televised victory that may have set standards for ugly basketball. So atrocious was the play on this Sunday afternoon that everyone from Rick Pitino to CBS-TV analyst Billy Packer was perplexed by the performances turned in by the two clubs, both of whom were ranked in the Top 10. The two teams combined for 58 turnovers, and neither shot better than 42 percent from the field (Syracuse 41.7 percent, UK 39.1 percent). Delk made just one of six three-point attempts, but it came with 3:20 left, squeezed between two Jeff Sheppard free throws and a Walter McCarty jam, and it highlighted a 13-4 rampage that broke open a 60-60 tie and gave the Cats a 73-64 lead. Also scoring for the Cats during this critical stretch were Antoine Walker

with a dunk and Rodrick Rhodes and McCarty with two free throws apiece. Syracuse, which trailed 29-24 at halftime, roared back to grab a 35-32 advantage. After a John Wallace bucket inside put Syracuse on top, 42-39, with 13:45 left to play, a three-point play by Mark Pope keyed an 11-0 run for UK. Pope's game-tying points were quickly followed by an

Anthony Epps trey, two Jared Prickett freebies and a Pope three-pointer. Eight points by Lawrence Moten brought the Orangemen back, tying the count at 62-62, before two Sheppard free throws, followed by Delk's three-pointer from the right side and a dunk by McCarty, gave UK the lead for good at 69-62 with 1:34 remaining.

Syracuse	fg-a	3-pt	ft-a	rb	a	b	pf	tp
Lucious Jackson	5-11	2-6	1-2	8	1	2	3	13
John Wallace	5-12	0-0	5-7	11	0	3	2	15
J.B. Reafsnyder	1-4	0-0	0-1	5	1	2	2	2
Michael Lloyd	1-8	0-1	0-0	4	2	0	2	2
Lawrence Moten	7-15	4-8	5-6	4	2	0	3	23
Lazarus Sims	2-4	0-0	1-2	2	2	0	3	5
Otis Hill	2-3	0-0	2-4	3	0	1	4	6
Todd Burgan	2-3	1-1	0-0	0	0	0	2	5
Team rebounds				4				
Totals	**25-60**	**7-16**	**14-22**	**41**	**8**	**8**	**21**	**71**

Kentucky	fg-a	3-pt	ft-a	rb	a	b	pf	tp
Rodrick Rhodes	0-3	0-1	4-4	4	6	1	1	4
Walter McCarty	4-10	1-2	6-6	9	1	1	2	15
Andre Riddick	4-6	0-0	3-4	5	1	2	4	11
Tony Delk	7-21	1-6	1-4	4	2	0	2	16
Jeff Sheppard	2-5	1-1	2-4	2	2	0	3	7
Mark Pope	3-6	1-2	1-2	6	0	1	3	8
Antoine Walker	3-7	0-1	3-4	4	1	0	1	9
Anthony Epps	2-4	1-2	0-0	2	1	0	2	5
Jared Prickett	0-2	0-0	2-2	2	1	0	2	2
Team rebounds				2				
Totals	**25-64**	**5-15**	**22-30**	**40**	**15**	**5**	**20**	**77**

Syracuse	24	47	—	71
Kentucky	29	48	—	77

Turnovers: Syracuse 33, Kentucky 25
Technicals: none
Officials: Jim Burr, Tim Higgins, John Cahill
Attendance: 24,225

1995 *Feb. 8*

Thompson-Boling Arena • Knoxville, Tenn.

Kentucky — 68
Tennessee — 48

W hen Tennessee's 7-0 center Steve Hamer went down with an injured knee, what might have been an interesting game suddenly turned into a classic example of men against boys. Hamer suffered his injury barely a minute into the game, and without him the Vols had no chance of knocking off the bigger, stronger and more talented Cats. With Hamer out, the Vols had but one player taller than 6-4. UK trailed early (14-7), but quickly righted itself by using an overpowering inside attack that the Vols were simply unable to stop. The Cats attempted 51 shots during the game, 27 of which came from within 10 feet of the bucket. In addition, Kentucky held an overwhelming 36-20 advantage in the rebounding department. Jared Prickett led the Cats' inside attack, scoring 15 points and snaring nine boards. Tony Delk topped UK's scoring with 19 points, and in the process became

the 42nd Wildcat to reach the career 1,000-point mark. Despite their sluggish start, the Cats, following an Antoine Walker dunk, a Delk three-pointer and back-to-back treys by Anthony Epps, were able to build a 39-24 lead by intermission. The second half featured more of the same, with the gritty Vols powerless to stop Kentucky

inside. UK's barrage of easy buckets translated into a 54.9 percent shooting night from the field. The lone bright spot for the Vols was junior Damon Johnson, who finished with 19 points. The win capped a season sweep of the Vols for Kentucky, having downed Tennessee by a similar margin of 69-50 two weeks earlier.

> "Just a bad game ... I don't think you can rate it. It was not a fun game to coach or a fun game to be part of."
>
> — Rick Pitino

Kentucky	fg-a	3-pt	ft-a	rb	a	b	pf	tp
Rodrick Rhodes	1-6	0-3	2-3	2	3	0	4	4
Walter McCarty	2-4	1-1	1-2	3	1	1	3	6
Andre Riddick	1-1	0-0	0-2	0	0	0	0	2
Tony Delk	7-14	2-4	3-3	3	1	0	1	19
Jeff Sheppard	1-2	0-1	0-0	2	1	0	0	2
Mark Pope	4-8	0-1	0-0	8	0	3	3	8
Jared Prickett	7-10	0-0	1-2	9	2	1	1	15
Anthony Epps	2-2	2-2	0-0	1	3	0	1	6
Antoine Walker	2-2	0-0	0-0	4	3	0	4	4
Chris Harrison	0-1	0-1	0-0	0	0	0	0	0
Allen Edwards	1-1	0-0	0-0	2	1	0	0	2
Team rebounds				2				
Totals	**28-51**	**5-13**	**7-12**	**36**	**15**	**5**	**17**	**68**

Tennessee	fg-a	3-pt	ft-a	rb	a	b	pf	tp
Damon Johnson	8-17	0-0	3-6	3	4	0	3	19
Shane Carnes	3-9	3-5	0-1	4	3	0	1	9
Steve Hamer	0-0	0-0	0-0	0	0	0	0	0
Alico Dunk	0-1	0-0	0-0	2	2	0	2	0
Shane Williams	5-11	2-4	0-0	5	3	0	0	12
Kevin Whitted	4-6	0-0	0-0	2	1	0	3	8
Jason Moore	0-2	0-1	0-0	1	1	0	1	0
Clint Newman	0-1	0-0	0-0	0	0	0	0	0
Team rebounds				3				
Totals	**20-47**	**5-10**	**3-7**	**20**	**14**	**0**	**10**	**48**

Kentucky	39	29 —	68
Tennessee	24	24 —	48

Turnovers: Tennessee 15, Kentucky 15
Technicals: none
Officials: Don Rutledge, André Pattillo, Mike Wood
Attendance: 22,317

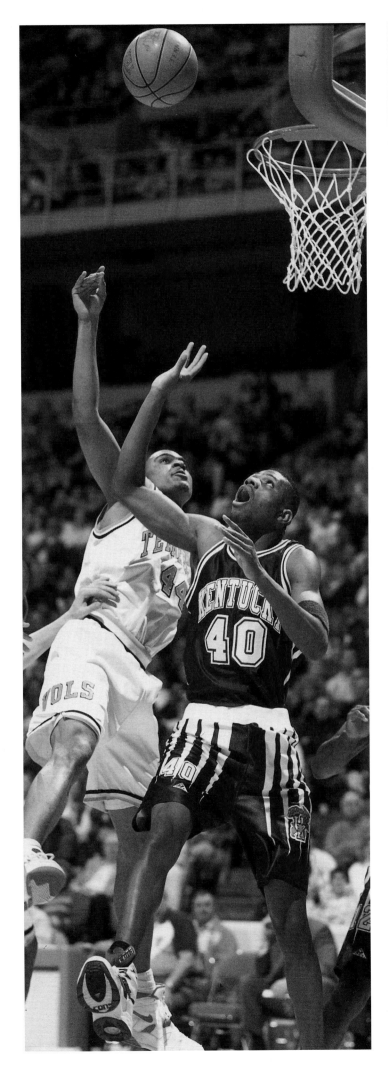

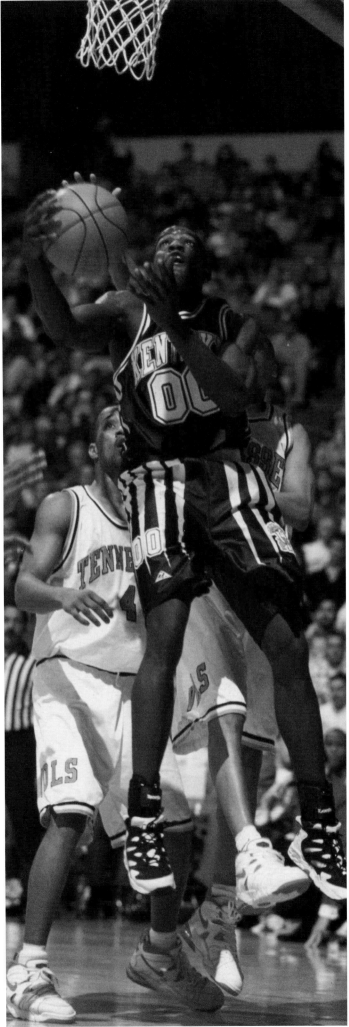

For more than a year now Derek Anderson has been an exile, living in a kind of basketball limbo located between memories of the past and dreams of the future.

Behind him are head-to-head clashes against such standout players as Calbert Cheaney, Jalen Rose and Jason Osborne; looming ahead is a future as a Kentucky Wildcat that offers endless and glorious possibilities.

For now, though, there is only the waiting and watching, the feeling of not belonging, of not being a part of what's happening. The feeling of not being a contributor.

And it's the waiting that gets you, Anderson says. The clock, ultimately, is a far more difficult opponent to deal with than mere mortals like Cheaney or Rose.

"Sitting out is very tough," Anderson said. "I knew it wasn't going to be easy, but it's even tougher than I thought it would be. I've sat out before, when I injured my knee, but that's not the same thing. I really can't explain it. I go to school and I practice. Then when it's game time, I'm just a spectator. It's not even like summer ball. Now I can't even compete, which is something I've done practically since I can remember."

Anderson hesitates, leans back in his chair, and smiles. There's a hint of twinkle in his eyes. Like a con artist who has successfully pulled off a tricky scam.

"It's been a long year," Anderson says, "but it's almost over. And I can't wait, either. I'm healthy for the first time in ages, and I'm filled with excitement and enthusiasm. I'm ready to get back at it."

Equally anxious and excited about the future is Rick Pitino, who was more than ready to accept Anderson into the Wildcat family when Anderson chose to transfer from Ohio State. That's not surprising, because Anderson is the prototypical Pitino player.

"Derek Anderson will bring many things to our basketball team," Pitino said. "He's a great athlete, he's intelligent, he's unselfish and his attitude is terrific. I would be really surprised if he doesn't have a great career at Kentucky."

Anderson's exile began when things came unraveled in Columbus. Several key players were suspended for disciplinary reasons, others chose to transfer. Chaos and uncertainty dominated the scene. It was, Anderson admits, a sad end to what had been a good two years.

"I loved it there," Anderson said, "and I really hated to leave. I liked playing for coach (Randy) Ayers, too. He's a great guy. But a lot of things were happening that were out of his control and out of my control. In the end, because of all that, and because I wanted to be closer to my daughter, I thought the best thing for me to do was to leave."

When word spread that Anderson was leaving Ohio State, it wasn't long before a flood of offers began pouring in. UCLA and Syracuse contacted him. So did Pittsburgh. Providence inquired.

But Anderson wasn't interested. He knew from the beginning that Kentucky was where he wanted to be.

"Actually, I called Coach Pitino in February," Anderson said, "but he told me he couldn't talk to me until I got my release. Once I did get it, the only possible hangup was my knee. He wanted to make sure it had healed properly."

UK put Anderson through a strenuous battery of tests. Once his surgically repaired knee received the thumbs up from team physician Dr. David Caborn, the deal was done.

Derek Anderson was officially a Kentucky Wildcat.

Why Kentucky? Several reasons, Anderson says.

"First, there's the family thing. My daughter, DeAsia, just turned one and I wanted to be in a position where I could see her more often. Second, I heard that Coach Pitino gets the best out of his players. That's what I wanted. And third, Kentucky's style of play suited me. Running, jumping, passing. Everything seemed to fit into place."

What UK fans can expect from Anderson is a proven commodity who possesses a vast array of basketball skills. In fact, versatility may be his strongest asset. During his two years at Ohio State, he played three positions — small forward, shooting guard and point guard. He had 166 assists and 180 rebounds. (That despite missing six games as a freshman and the final seven games of his sophomore season.) And on the defensive end, it wasn't unusual for him to be paired off against the opponent's best scorer.

In short, Anderson brings the total package to UK.

Anderson's success at Ohio State came as a surprise to no one. He'd been an all-state performer at Louisville Doss High School, averaging 24 points and 10 rebounds during his senior year. He was the most valuable player at the 1993 Olympic Festival. (His future UK teammate Jared Prickett also per-

Wildcat in Waiting

formed splendidly at that event.) Then came his two solid seasons with the Buckeyes, where, as a sophomore, he ranked among the league's top 10 in three statistical categories.

Included among Anderson's finest efforts was a 23-point performance in a 100-88 loss to UK at the Maui Classic. He also had 20 points and nine rebounds in a victory over Indiana.

Ironically, UK showed little interest in recruiting Anderson out of high school. But unlike those legions of Kentucky kids who dream of playing for the Big Blue, Anderson wasn't at all bothered by UK's indifference.

"It was no big deal to me," he said. "I guess that's because I'm not originally from Kentucky. I'm from Flint, Michigan. My family didn't move to Louisville until I was 10, so I really didn't know much about UK. In those days, my favorite teams were the Pistons and Michigan."

Along with versatile and consistent, one other adjective comes to mind when describing Anderson's game — efficient. Little, if anything, is wasted or unfocused. Consider his sophomore numbers at Ohio State. He averaged 15 points, yet he took just 10 shots per game.

But all of that is in the past. Scrapbook stuff that seems a million years ago. For now there is only the waiting. The

Anderson spent this season rooting his teammates on from the bench.

Shown here playing for Ohio State, Anderson brings his versatile game to Kentucky.

waiting, listening and learning.

"What I mostly do at practice now is take notes in my head," Anderson said. "Basketball is 90 percent mental and 10 percent physical, so if you want to be successful, you'd better be as smart as you are talented. That's why I try to pick up and absorb everything the coaches tell us. If I do, then that should make things easier for me next year. And, of course, I continually keep working on my skills."

Ah, next year. Anderson doesn't even attempt to conceal his joy when asked about the possibilities for next year's team.

"Oh, I really believe that we'll have a real strong team," he says. "We'll have a lot of experience. If you look at our team, it's hard to find many weaknesses. We should definitely challenge for the national championship."

And what does Anderson think he'll bring to that team?

"A lot, I hope," he says. "I feel like I can help the team at three different positions. I think I can play several roles. It's just a matter of where the coaches want me to play. I'll do whatever they ask me to do."

Again the smile.

"I can't wait to put on a uniform once again," he says. "This watching and waiting gets old in a hurry."

Notre Dame
The Kentucky Game
February 12, 1995

KEITH KUROWSKI

Kentucky 97
Notre Dame 58

"I kept getting good looks at the basket and my shots were going down. What can I say? I played great today."

— Walter McCarty

alter McCarty is known as "Ice" to his teammates, but if you asked the Notre Dame players, they might be inclined to call him "Fire." As in on fire from just about every conceivable spot in the Joyce Center, an arena that traditionally hasn't been all that kind to highly ranked visitors. But any notion of another in a long line of classic Irish upsets was quickly put to rest by McCarty, whose sizzling shooting iced this game for the Cats before the leprechauns had a chance to work their magic. He scored UK's first five points, 12 of the first 16, and he had 17 by halftime, which ended with the Cats holding a commanding 45-29 lead. During that decisive 20 minutes, UK made good on 16 attempts. So dominating was the UK defense that Notre Dame managed only 14 field goals all afternoon. Not surprisingly, the result was Notre Dame's worst home loss since 1898, and its worst loss anywhere

since losing to UK 100-53 in 1971. The Cats were able to hammer Notre Dame so easily because they combined their trademark "D" with some hot shooting and sharp passing. For the game, Kentucky shot 53.4 percent from the field and had 23 assists. The only black mark on this UK perfor-

mance was the 19 turnovers. Six Wildcats hit double figures, led by McCarty's 20. Tony Delk, Antoine Walker and Jared Prickett each scored 13 points, Anthony Epps had 11 and Jeff Sheppard added 10. UK also owned the boards, winning that battle by a convincing 39-24 margin.

Kentucky	fg-a	3-pt	ft-a	rb	a	b	pf	tp
Rodrick Rhodes	1-7	0-2	1-2	6	5	0	4	3
Walter McCarty	7-12	4-6	2-2	7	4	1	1	20
Andre Riddick	1-3	0-0	1-1	4	0	0	4	3
Tony Delk	5-8	3-6	0-2	1	2	0	2	13
Jeff Sheppard	3-5	0-1	4-4	0	5	0	3	10
Chris Harrison	2-4	2-4	0-0	1	0	0	2	6
Cameron Mills	0-1	0-1	0-0	0	0	0	0	0
Allen Edwards	1-1	1-1	0-0	1	0	0	0	3
Antoine Walker	3-5	0-2	7-8	9	2	0	4	13
Anthony Epps	2-3	2-2	5-6	2	3	0	1	11
Jared Prickett	6-8	0-0	1-1	5	2	0	1	13
Scott Padgett	0-1	0-1	2-2	2	0	1	1	2
Mark Pope	0-0	0-0	0-0	0	0	0	4	0
Team rebounds				1				
Totals	31-58	12-26	23-28	39	23	2	27	97

Notre Dame	fg-a	3-pt	ft-a	rb	a	b	pf	tp
Jason Williams	2-3	0-1	0-1	1	0	0	3	4
Pat Garrity	1-8	0-1	5-8	2	0	0	1	7
Marcus Young	3-3	0-0	0-0	2	0	1	4	6
Ryan Hoover	3-5	1-3	5-6	0	0	0	2	12
Lamarr Justice	1-4	0-0	1-2	4	6	0	4	3
Derek Manner	2-7	1-1	7-8	3	0	0	0	12
Admore White	1-2	1-1	3-4	1	1	0	3	6
Keith Kurowski	0-1	0-0	1-2	0	1	0	0	1
Pete Miller	0-1	0-0	2-2	0	0	0	2	2
Billy Taylor	0-1	0-0	2-3	0	0	0	0	2
Matt Gotsch	1-2	0-0	0-0	3	0	0	2	2
Brian Watkins	0-5	0-0	1-4	4	1	1	2	1
Team rebounds				4				
Totals	14-42	3-7	27-40	24	9	2	23	58

Kentucky	45	52	—	97
Notre Dame	29	29	—	58

Turnovers: Notre Dame 23, Kentucky 19
Technicals: Kentucky — Riddick; Notre Dame — Williams
Officials: Frank Scagliotta, Edwin Edsall, Rick Hartzell
Attendance: 11,418

KENTUCKY
Swish Magazine

Allen Edwards
Here's the Scoop

1995

Feb. 14

Rupp Arena • Lexington, Ky.

Mississippi St. 76
Kentucky 71

"Mississippi State was the better team from start to finish. We've got no excuses except to say we got beat by a better team ... Mississippi State is a big-time ballclub."

— Rick Pitino

Mississippi State stole a page from Kentucky's trademark basketball textbook, using the three-pointer to demoralize an opponent, and the result was the Bulldogs' first victory in Lexington since 1967. But perhaps even more impressive was the Bulldogs' mental toughness. Unlike in past years, when victory seemed within their grasp, this time the Bulldogs stared UK in the face and refused to blink. Time after time, State players consistently came up with big plays to take the air out of UK's repeated comeback attempts. Thanks to monster performances by Marcus Grant and Erick Dampier, the result was State's biggest win in years. Shooting, both from the field and the charity stripe, proved to be the difference. UK took 33 more shots than the Bulldogs (80-47) and won the rebounding battle (38-32), but those advantages were neutralized by State's excellent shooting. State made good on 27 of 47 shots (57.4 percent), including 11 of 20 from three-point range. In addition, the Bulldogs were 11 of 16 from the free throw line. By contrast, the Cats connected on 29 field goals for a cool 36.3 percent, and went to the free throw line just six times, making four. UK led on four occasions, the last of which came when a Rodrick Rhodes layup made it 39-38 with 19:57 remaining. But when Marcus Bullard countered with a trey 11 seconds later, the Bulldogs had a lead they refused to surrender despite repeated UK threats. Grant hit six of eight three-point attempts and led State with 23 points. Dampier finished with 17 points and 13 rebounds. Tony Delk topped UK in scoring with 16 points.

Mississippi St.	fg-a	3-pt	ft-a	rb	a	b	pf	tp
Marcus Grant	8-14	6-8	1-1	5	7	4	2	23
Marcus Bullard	5-7	2-4	3-4	2	2	0	2	15
Erick Dampier	7-9	0-0	3-4	13	3	1	3	17
Darryl Wilson	4-10	3-7	2-5	2	3	0	3	13
T.J. Honore	3-6	0-1	2-2	2	3	0	2	8
Russell Walters	0-1	0-0	0-0	0	0	0	1	0
Whit Hughes	0-0	0-0	0-0	2	1	0	1	0
Jay Walton	0-0	0-0	0-0	0	1	0	0	0
Team rebounds				6				
Totals	**27-47**	**11-20**	**11-16**	**32**	**20**	**5**	**14**	**76**

Kentucky	fg-a	3-pt	ft-a	rb	a	b	pf	tp
Rodrick Rhodes	6-17	1-6	2-2	7	2	0	2	15
Walter McCarty	4-10	0-2	0-0	6	1	0	4	8
Andre Riddick	0-0	0-0	0-0	0	0	1	3	0
Tony Delk	5-13	4-11	2-2	4	3	0	1	16
Jeff Sheppard	4-13	1-7	0-1	4	2	0	2	9
Anthony Epps	2-11	1-4	0-0	2	4	0	0	5
Mark Pope	5-6	2-2	0-0	8	3	3	4	12
Jared Prickett	2-7	0-1	0-1	4	2	0	1	4
Antoine Walker	1-3	0-1	0-0	0	0	0	1	2
Team rebounds				3				
Totals	**29-80**	**9-34**	**4-6**	**38**	**17**	**4**	**18**	**71**

Mississippi State	38	38 —	76
Kentucky	37	34 —	71

Turnovers: Mississippi St. 24, Kentucky 11
Technicals: none
Officials: Frank Scagliotta, Jim Burr, André Pattillo
Attendance: 24,125

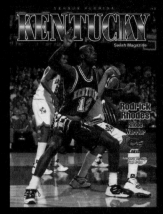

KENTUCKY
Swish Magazine

Rodrick Rhodes
Rhoda Warrior

1995

Feb. 18

Rupp Arena • Lexington, Ky.

| Florida | 77 |
| Kentucky | 87 |

"Chris (Harrison) gave us a big lift when we really needed it. And Rod (Rhodes) was spectacular. He had one of his best games today."

— Rick Pitino

"Usually when I hit my first shot, I know I'm going to have a good shooting game. That's what happened today. When that first three-pointer went down, I said to myself, 'OK, I can help this team today.'"

— Chris Harrison

ith three-time heavyweight boxing champion Muhammad Ali watching from the bench, Rodrick Rhodes and Chris Harrison delivered a solid one-two punch that had a tough bunch of Gators reeling from the ropes when the final bell sounded. Rhodes came up big, scoring 23 points, grabbing six rebounds and playing smothering defense, while Harrison, the senior from Tollesboro, used his long-range gunning to pick the Cats up off the canvas just when thoughts of a second straight home loss were beginning to stir among the Rupp Arena throng. Florida, spurred by Dan Cross' 16 points, owned the first half, building a lead that once stretched to 11 points (32-21), and had it not been for Rhodes, who scored his team's first seven points against a tricky match-up zone, the Gators likely would have had UK down for the count. But just when things looked bleakest for Kentucky,

Harrison stroked a trey that lit a fire under his teammates and woke up the sleeping Rupp Arena crowd. Walter McCarty scored UK's next four points to complete a 7-0 run that put the Cats back into the hunt. The Gators led 40-33 at intermission. The second half saw 10 lead changes, and it wasn't until Jared Prickett hit a jumper

with 3:59 left that UK took the lead for good at 72-71. With 1:23 left, Harrison replaced a bloodied Jeff Sheppard and hit two freebies to give UK a 79-75 lead. Rhodes then delivered the knockout blows, first by hitting a leaner in the lane, then by stripping the ball from Cross, drawing a foul and sinking two free throws.

Florida	fg-a	3-pt	ft-a	rb	a	b	pf	tp
Brian Thompson	1-2	0-0	0-0	2	0	0	2	2
Andrew DeClercq	8-11	0-1	6-9	7	1	2	3	22
Dametri Hill	5-11	0-0	2-2	7	1	2	5	12
Greg Williams	2-7	1-2	2-2	3	5	0	1	7
Dan Cross	7-13	0-1	16-16	5	5	0	4	30
Jason Anderson	1-1	0-0	0-0	3	1	1	4	2
LeRon Williams	1-2	0-0	0-0	1	0	1	1	2
Dan Williams	0-0	0-0	0-0	1	0	0	0	0
John Griffiths	0-0	0-0	0-0	1	0	0	0	0
Team rebounds				3				
Totals	25-47	1-4	26-29	33	13	6	20	77

Kentucky	fg-a	3-pt	ft-a	rb	a	b	pf	tp
Rodrick Rhodes	7-15	1-3	8-11	6	4	0	4	23
Walter McCarty	2-9	0-4	2-2	5	1	0	4	6
Andre Riddick	1-1	0-0	0-0	0	0	0	3	2
Tony Delk	7-14	3-6	2-2	4	2	0	4	19
Jeff Sheppard	2-5	0-1	0-0	1	6	1	4	4
Mark Pope	3-5	2-3	6-7	4	2	4	1	14
Anthony Epps	1-7	0-2	0-0	1	3	0	0	2
Antoine Walker	0-3	0-0	0-1	2	0	0	1	0
Jared Prickett	3-6	0-0	0-2	6	1	1	1	6
Chris Harrison	3-6	3-6	2-2	1	0	0	0	11
Team rebounds				4				
Totals	29-71	9-25	20-27	34	19	6	22	87

Florida	40	37 —	77
Kentucky	33	54 —	87

Turnovers: Florida 22, Kentucky 9
Technicals: none
Officials: Gene Monje, Kerry Sitton, Tom Eades
Attendance: 24,320

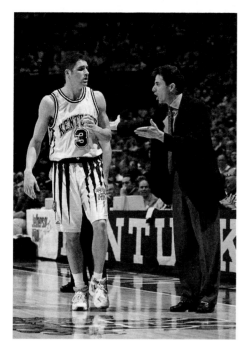

1995 *Feb. 21* Coleman Coliseum • Tuscaloosa, Ala.

Kentucky 72
Alabama 52

"Once again our defense was outstanding. We were brilliant mentally as well as physically."

— Rick Pitino

"The spin move ... something new? Nah, not really. I used to practice it all the time — until my teammates started getting on me."

— Walter McCarty

D efense, this UK team's most consistent area, reached its high-water mark of the season in this surprisingly easy win over 20th-ranked Alabama in Tuscaloosa. The Cats, using mainly a match-up zone, held the Tide to a season low in points scored and a near-season low in field goal percentage (30.3). During one span midway through the first half, Alabama, which shot an anemic 23 percent from the field in the opening stanza, went nearly nine minutes without scoring a basket. UK, meanwhile, ran off 19 points to assume control. By the time the Tide finally broke the ice, UK was sitting on a 28-13 lead. The Cats were on top 33-20 at the half. Junior Walter McCarty keyed the Cats during those opening 20 minutes, using a variety of acrobatic, spinning moves to rack up 12 points. His back-to-back buckets erased Alabama's 12-10 lead and sent the Cats on their decisive 18-1 explosion. The Tide

threatened to make several runs in the second half, but each one was answered by UK. Mark Pope's tip-in put Kentucky's lead at 48-32, and moments later, Chris Harrison's trey extended the Cats' margin to 53-35. If the first half was a showcase for McCarty, then the second half belonged to Rodrick

Rhodes and Tony Delk. When 'Bama closed to within 10 on a three-pointer by Marvin Orange, Delk converted a three-point play and Rhodes rammed in a dunk to turn the momentum back in UK's favor. Rhodes ended up as UK's leading scorer with 16 points. McCarty and Delk each had 14.

Kentucky	fg-a	3-pt	ft-a	rb	a	b	pf	tp
Rodrick Rhodes	4-11	0-1	8-8	8	2	0	2	16
Walter McCarty	7-12	0-3	0-1	8	0	2	3	14
Tony Delk	6-10	1-4	1-2	5	1	0	0	14
Jeff Sheppard	1-4	0-0	4-4	1	2	0	3	6
Andre Riddick	2-6	0-0	0-0	3	1	2	4	4
Chris Harrison	2-5	2-4	0-0	1	1	0	0	6
Allen Edwards	0-0	0-0	0-0	0	0	0	0	0
Antoine Walker	0-1	0-1	0-0	0	0	0	0	0
Anthony Epps	0-0	0-0	0-0	0	0	0	0	0
Jared Prickett	2-5	0-0	2-4	0	3	0	2	6
Mark Pope	2-3	0-0	2-2	7	1	0	2	6
Team rebounds				4				
Totals	26-57	3-13	17-21	37	11	4	16	72

Alabama	fg-a	3-pt	ft-a	rb	a	b	pf	tp
Jamal Faulkner	3-15	2-9	1-2	8	2	0	0	9
Jason Caffey	5-11	0-0	3-10	9	0	0	1	13
Marvin Orange	2-4	2-4	0-0	0	3	0	0	6
Artie Griffin	2-5	2-5	1-2	6	2	0	3	7
Antonio McDyess	6-15	0-0	0-2	11	0	1	5	12
Terrance Bethel	0-1	0-1	0-0	1	1	0	0	0
Marco Whitfield	0-2	0-2	0-0	1	4	0	1	0
Eric Washington	0-7	0-6	0-0	0	1	0	1	0
Bryan Passink	1-3	1-2	0-0	2	1	0	3	3
Scott Hamilton	0-0	0-0	0-0	0	0	0	0	0
Roy Rogers	1-3	0-0	0-0	4	1	5	1	2
Team rebounds				6				
Totals	20-66	7-29	5-16	48	15	6	15	52

Kentucky 33	39	—	72
Alabama....................................20	32	—	52

Turnovers: Alabama 17, Kentucky 10
Technicals: none
Officials: John Clougherty, Jim Burr, Gene Monje
Attendance: 15,043

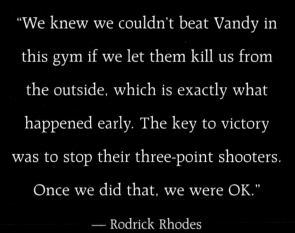

1995

Feb. 25

Memorial Gym • Nashville, Tenn.

Kentucky 71
Vanderbilt 60

"We knew we couldn't beat Vandy in this gym if we let them kill us from the outside, which is exactly what happened early. The key to victory was to stop their three-point shooters. Once we did that, we were OK."

— Rodrick Rhodes

An early 20-second timeout, steady play by Tony Delk, timely three-pointers by Mark Pope and Walter McCarty and, of course, that old standby, defense, helped propel the Cats to their come-from-behind victory in Music City. The win was the 20th of the season for the Cats, thus marking the fifth time in Rick Pitino's six-year stint as head coach that he has guided UK to the celebrated 20-victory plateau. The win didn't come easily, and it didn't come without a struggle. With Ronnie McMahan opening on fire, hitting three straight three-pointers, Vandy ran out to a 16-6 lead less than seven minutes into the game. It was then that Pitino called the 20-second timeout that proved to be the turning point for the Cats, who quickly got their defensive act in gear, especially when it came to stopping the Commodores' long-range bombing. After Pitino issued

a blistering challenge to his players to tighten the reins on McMahan, just two of the superb Vandy senior's next eight missiles found their mark. Delk was the chief architect of UK's comeback, and when he scored on a rebound bucket after a Pope miss, the Cats had drawn even at 22-22. Vandy pushed ahead 29-24 by half-

time, and that lead could have been bigger had Vandy not gone an uncharacteristic one-for-five from the free throw line. The second half was all UK, thanks to the big plays turned in by Pope, Delk and McCarty, and a defense that held Vandy to just three field goals in the final 10 minutes. Delk led all scorers with 22 points.

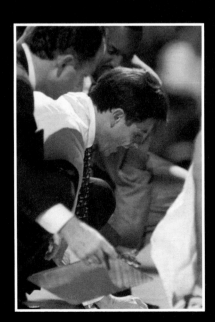

Kentucky	fg-a	3-pt	ft-a	rb	a	b	pf	tp
Rodrick Rhodes	4-10	2-5	2-4	4	2	0	3	12
Walter McCarty	2-8	1-3	3-4	9	2	1	3	8
Tony Delk	8-17	0-5	6-6	5	1	0	1	22
Jeff Sheppard	2-4	1-2	2-3	4	2	1	3	7
Andre Riddick	2-5	0-0	0-1	3	0	1	4	4
Chris Harrison	0-0	0-0	0-0	0	0	0	0	0
Antoine Walker	1-4	0-1	0-0	1	0	0	2	2
Anthony Epps	0-1	0-1	0-0	3	0	0	1	0
Jared Prickett	1-1	0-0	2-2	4	1	0	1	4
Mark Pope	5-8	1-2	1-2	6	1	0	2	12
Team rebounds				4				
Totals	25-58	5-19	16-22	43	9	3	20	71

Vanderbilt	fg-a	3-pt	ft-a	rb	a	b	pf	tp
Ronnie McMahan	6-18	5-11	0-3	3	2	0	3	17
Bryan Milburn	3-6	0-0	0-0	5	3	0	3	6
Chris Woods	3-5	0-0	0-0	5	1	6	2	6
Frank Seckar	5-9	1-3	0-2	3	5	0	2	11
Drew Maddux	2-7	1-2	1-2	4	2	0	3	6
Chad Sheron	0-0	0-0	0-0	0	0	0	0	0
Howard Pride	0-1	0-0	2-4	2	0	0	3	2
J.J. Lucas	2-3	0-0	2-2	2	1	0	1	6
Malik Evans	2-2	0-0	2-4	4	0	0	1	6
Team rebounds				2				
Totals	23-51	7-16	7-17	30	14	6	18	60

Kentucky	24	47 —	71
Vanderbilt	29	31 —	60

Turnovers: Vanderbilt 14, Kentucky 13
Technicals: none
Officials: Rusty Herring, David Dodge, Mike Thibodeaux
Attendance: 15,208

Taking a trip with the Wildcats is at once an exciting and hectic experience. It is first-class, luxurious, crowded and chaotic. In short, it's everything you would expect when an entourage consisting of 50-plus people goes on a trip. As a general rule the team stays overnight, although in recent years that has not always been the case. Because of television-dictated 9:30 p.m. games, it's not unusual for the trip to be a same-day deal. Usually, though, the team will practice at Memorial Coliseum, then board a bus for Blue Grass Field, where a charter plane is waiting. Box lunches on the plane are standard fare. Upon arriving and checking into the motel, if it's not too late, the players and coaches congregate in a banquet room to watch film and discuss strategy. Game day begins at about 9 a.m. with breakfast and more film work. Then it's off to the opponent's arena for what most teams term a walk-through, but for UK is really another practice. After practice, it's back to the motel, where the players can always expect to be greeted by a throng of Big Blue supporters. The players relax until it's time for the pre-game meal. After eating and watching more film, Coach Pitino writes the keys to victory on a chalkboard, then goes over each one in detail. Nothing is left to chance. The bus ride to the arena is always a quiet, contemplative time. No laughing, no cutting up ... it's serious business for everyone. The mood on the plane during the trip back to Lexington depends on the outcome of the game and the level of performance. A great effort gets everyone upbeat, while a poor performance, even in victory, translates into a downer. Either way, the players can always count on one thing — another box lunch.

CATS

On the Road with the

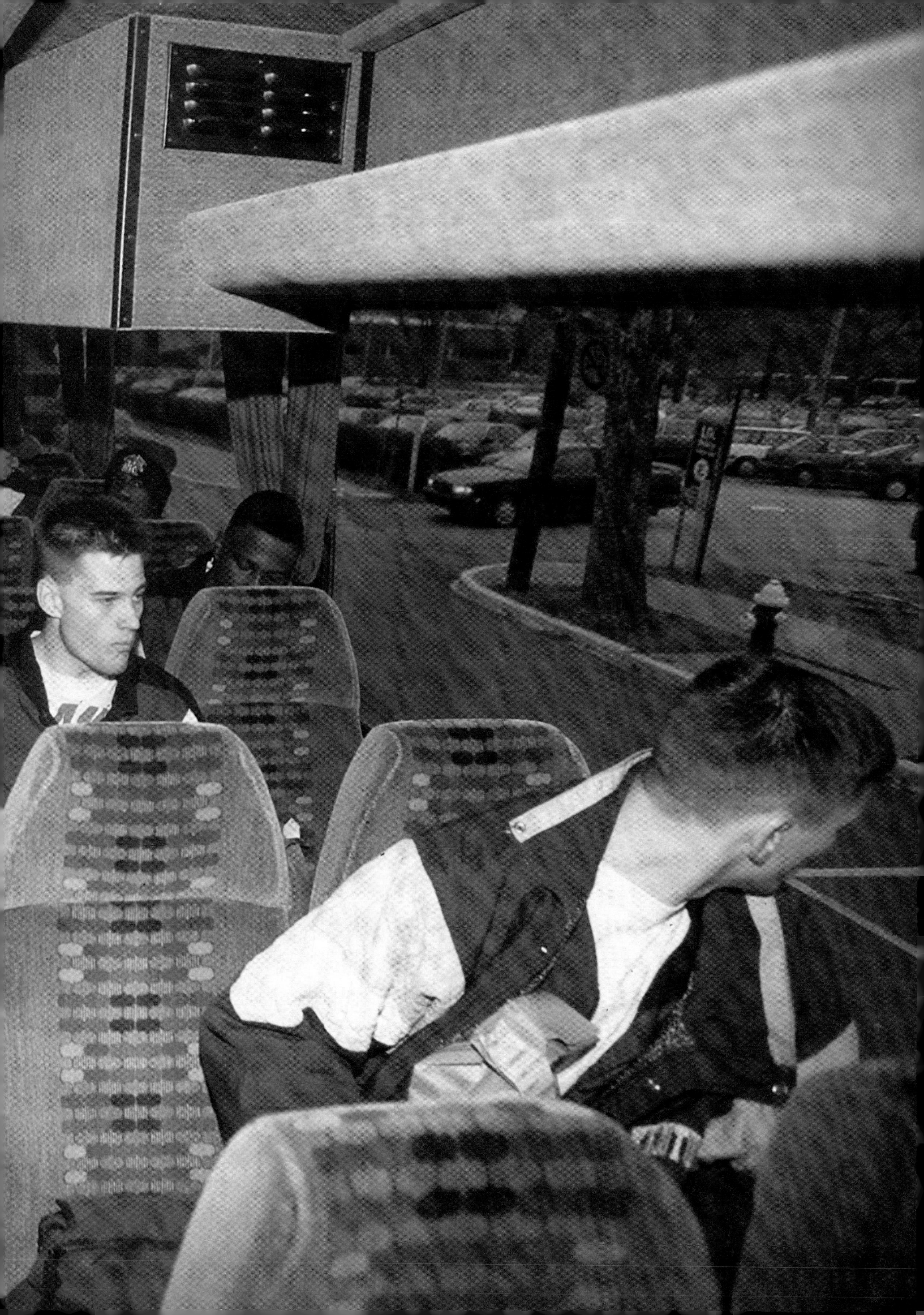

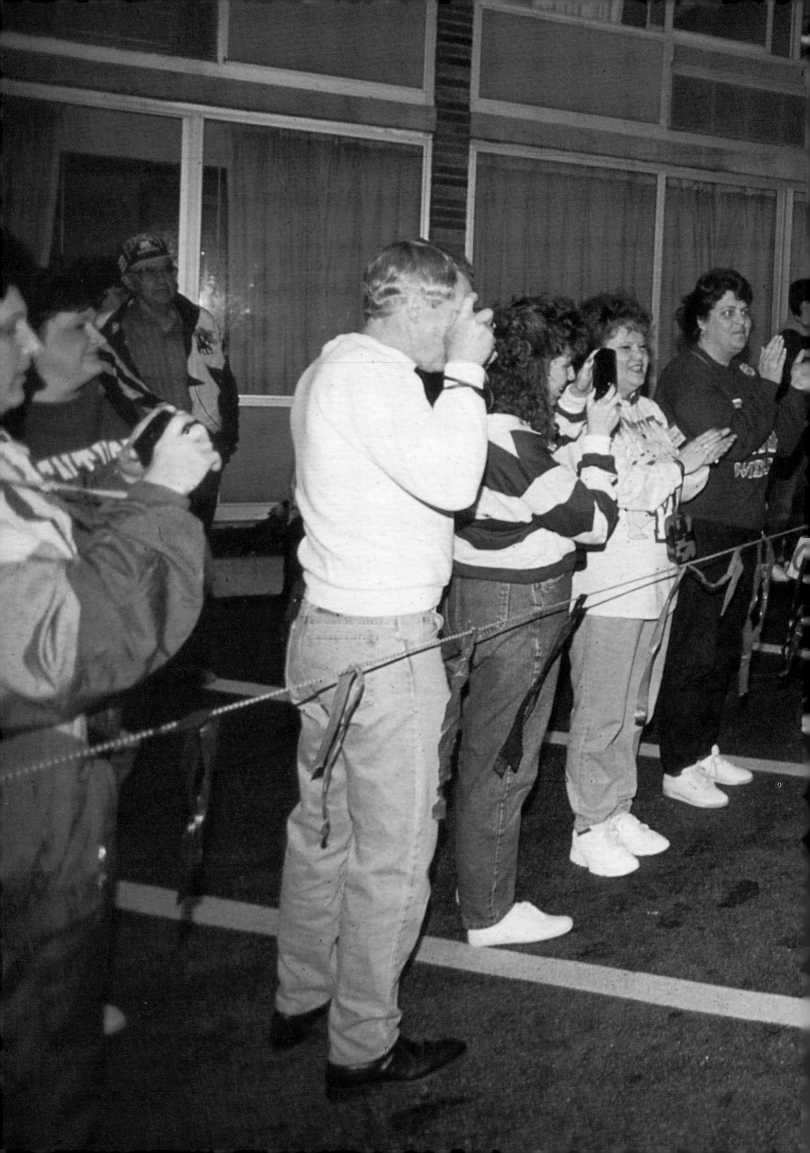

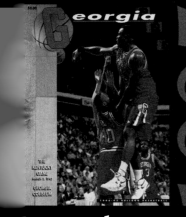

1995

March 1

Georgia Coliseum • Athens, Ga.

Kentucky 97
Georgia 74

"We had to win three very, very tough road games to accomplish our goals. We did that. And we did it in high fashion. Our offense was great. Our defense was great. Our press was terrific."

— Rick Pitino

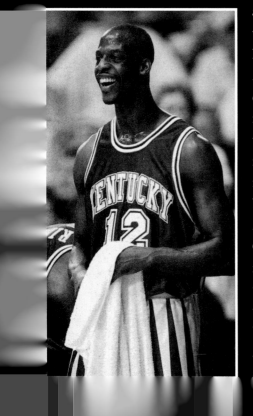

UK completed a hugely successful three-game road swing by surgically carving up the Bulldogs, and in the process, captured the school's 37th Southeastern Conference regular-season championship. During that three-game sweep, the Cats beat Alabama, Vanderbilt and Georgia by a combined total of 54 points. The 23-point margin was UK's easiest victory at Georgia since 1948. It also provided Hugh Durham with his worst home loss in his 17 seasons at Georgia. After an ugly start by both clubs (the score was 11-6 for more than three minutes), UK went on an 11-4 run that made it 22-10 with 7:36 left in the half. The Dawgs, behind six Shandon Anderson points and a Charles Claxton dunk, mounted their only real threat of the night, closing to within 24-18 with 6:18 left before the break. But UK, after a 20-second time out, quickly slammed the door on

Georgia's hopes by scoring nine unanswered points — seven by Tony Delk and two by Rodrick Rhodes — to take a 33-18 lead. The Cats received a big boost from Anthony Epps, who scored eight points in 13 minutes of first-half action. Epps was pressed into duty when a Bulldog elbow opened a cut

over Jeff Sheppard's eye that required five stitches to close. Georgia threatened to make things interesting, whittling the difference to 11 (58-47), but the threat turned out to be little more than a weak bluff. UK exploded, scoring 10 points in less than two minutes to turn a potential thriller into a blowout.

Kentucky	fg-a	3-pt	ft-a	rb	a	b	pf	tp
Rodrick Rhodes	5-6	0-0	5-7	4	1	0	2	15
Walter McCarty	3-7	1-2	3-5	4	4	2	2	10
Andre Riddick	6-7	0-0	2-4	3	0	0	4	14
Tony Delk	7-14	1-4	1-3	5	5	0	2	16
Jeff Sheppard	3-11	0-3	4-5	2	3	0	3	10
Chris Harrison	0-0	0-0	0-0	1	1	0	1	0
Allen Edwards	0-0	0-0	0-0	0	0	0	0	0
Antoine Walker	2-5	1-2	6-7	7	0	0	2	11
Anthony Epps	3-4	2-2	0-0	2	1	0	1	8
Jared Prickett	4-6	0-0	0-0	1	1	0	2	8
Scott Padgett	0-2	0-0	0-0	0	0	0	2	0
Mark Pope	2-4	1-2	0-0	4	3	0	4	5
Team rebounds				4				
Totals	**35-66**	**6-15**	**21-31**	**37**	**19**	**2**	**25**	**97**

Georgia	fg-a	3-pt	ft-a	rb	a	b	pf	tp
Carlos Strong	5-13	0-1	11-15	9	1	0	3	21
Shandon Anderson	3-14	1-3	2-9	6	1	0	3	9
Charles Claxton	2-5	0-0	4-6	8	0	1	4	8
Pertha Robinson	1-4	0-1	0-1	5	3	0	2	2
Katu Davis	4-10	1-5	4-5	6	6	0	3	13
Ty Wilson	0-0	0-0	0-0	0	0	0	2	0
Steve Jones	2-4	0-0	0-0	2	1	0	0	4
Curtis Carrington	4-8	1-4	0-0	4	0	0	2	9
Terrell Bell	4-4	0-0	0-0	3	0	1	4	8
Team rebounds				4				
Totals	**25-62**	**3-14**	**21-36**	**47**	**12**	**2**	**23**	**74**

Kentucky	40	57 —	97
Georgia	26	48 —	74

Turnovers: Georgia 19, Kentucky 11
Technicals: none
Officials: John Clougherty, Joe Mingle, Curtis Shaw
Attendance: 10,523

WILDCAT SENIOR

★

ANDRE RIDDICK

10

KENTUCKY SENIOR DAY

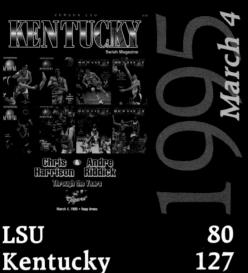

VERSUS LSU

KENTUCKY
Swish Magazine

Chris &   Andre
Harrison Riddick
Through the Years

Tigers
March 4, 1995 • Rupp Arena

1995

March 4

Rupp Arena • Lexington, Ky.

LSU   80
Kentucky   127

"This was the old days. We have not been a three-point shooting team. We've relied on dribble penetration and getting the ball inside. Tonight, we got hot."

— Rick Pitino

"This was certainly a very special day for me. If I had been able to write a script, this is exactly how I would have written it."

— Chris Harrison

hris Harrison's sense of timing couldn't have been better. Playing his final game in Rupp Arena, the 6-1 Tollesboro native gave the best performance of his UK career, scoring 16 points as the Cats made a shambles of Dale Brown's Tigers. Harrison's outside gunning also helped the Cats set a host of records, including most points scored in Rupp Arena, most three-pointers made by Kentucky in Rupp Arena and in an SEC game (20), best three-point shooting accuracy (57.1 percent) and largest margin of victory over LSU (47 points). In every way, it was a fitting farewell for seniors Harrison and Andre Riddick. But it didn't start off that way. The Cats struggled early, finding themselves on the short end of a 19-17 score after LSU's Clarence Ceasar rung up four straight points, and it wasn't until Tony Delk hit the first of two straight three-pointers that the Cats were off and running. During the final 10 minutes of the

half, UK sizzled, connecting on 15 of its next 19 shots. The Cats were especially hot from behind the three-point arc, making good on 12 of 18 first-half trey attempts. Late in the half, Harrison electrified the crowd — and demolished LSU — by hitting three treys in a 60-second span. When he finished his barrage, UK was

leading 55-31. Harrison's dramatic explosion almost overshadowed Delk's 21 first-half points. The second half was little more than a repeat of the first 20 minutes, with Kentucky seemingly able to score at will against the porous LSU defense. By game's end, seven Wildcats had made at least one trey.

LSU	fg-a	3-pt	ft-a	rb	a	b	pf	tp
Landers Nolley	0-9	0-1	1-2	8	1	1	3	1
Quenton Thomas	0-2	0-1	0-0	0	4	0	4	0
Ronnie Henderson	8-18	2-4	4-6	3	0	0	4	22
Clarence Ceasar	8-17	4-9	4-6	7	5	0	3	24
Roman Rubchenko	8-14	2-5	2-4	7	1	0	4	20
Garrick Scott	1-5	0-0	2-5	3	0	0	0	4
David Bosley	1-2	1-1	0-0	1	5	0	0	3
Misha Mutavdzic	0-1	0-0	2-3	2	0	0	3	2
Alonzo Johnson	1-1	0-0	0-0	0	0	0	1	2
Djole Palfi	1-2	0-0	0-0	1	0	0	0	2
Team rebounds				5				
Totals	**28-71**	**9-21**	**15-26**	**37**	**16**	**1**	**22**	**80**

Kentucky	fg-a	3-pt	ft-a	rb	a	b	pf	tp
Rodrick Rhodes	6-10	3-3	2-2	2	4	0	2	17
Walter McCarty	3-5	0-1	4-6	4	1	1	2	10
Andre Riddick	3-7	0-3	3-6	9	0	5	4	9
Tony Delk	8-12	6-8	5-5	0	0	0	3	27
Jeff Sheppard	2-5	0-0	0-0	2	4	1	1	4
Antoine Walker	4-7	2-4	1-1	6	1	2	1	11
Mark Pope	1-3	1-1	4-4	3	0	0	2	7
Anthony Epps	4-5	3-4	4-4	5	13	0	2	15
Jared Prickett	3-4	0-0	0-0	4	2	0	1	6
Chris Harrison	5-10	4-9	2-2	1	2	0	3	16
Allen Edwards	0-1	0-0	0-0	0	1	0	0	0
Scott Padgett	2-2	1-1	0-0	4	2	0	2	5
Cameron Mills	0-1	0-1	0-2	0	1	0	0	0
Team rebounds				1				
Team	**41-72**	**20-35**	**25-32**	**41**	**31**	**9**	**23**	**127**

LSU	36	44	—	80
Kentucky	63	64	—	127

Turnovers: LSU 22, Kentucky 15
Technicals: LSU — Quenton Thomas
Officials: Rusty Herring, Tom Lopes, George Washington
Attendance: 24,325

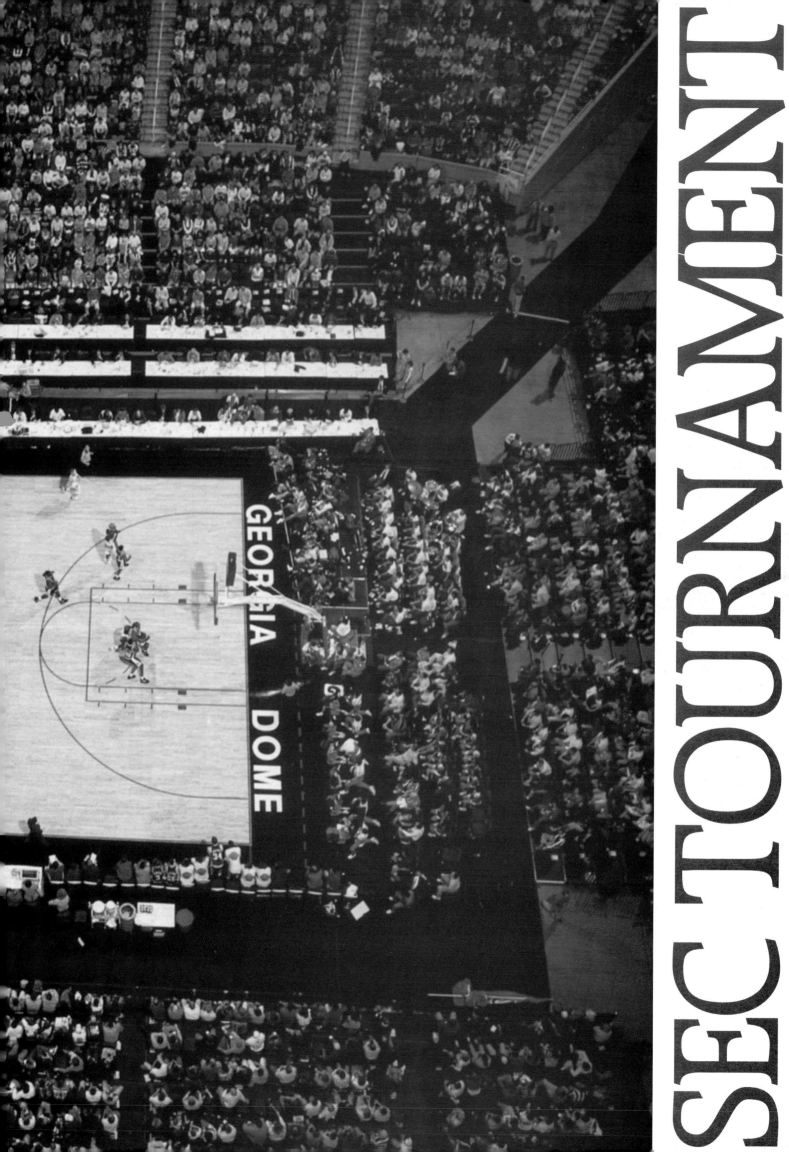

SEC TOURNAMENT

Auburn 81
Kentucky 93

"For 32 minutes, we played great basketball. We played good defense, we took good shots and we attacked their press. But in the last eight minutes, we lost our concentration, and that's something you can't do in the NCAA Tournament."

— Rick Pitino

"When Kentucky had that big lead on us, I kept thinking back to last season when they came from 31 points down against LSU and won the game."

— (Auburn guard) Moochie Norris

Walter McCarty and Mark Pope combined for 41 points and 20 rebounds to power the Cats past Auburn in SEC tourney quarterfinal action. McCarty scored 22 points and had 10 rebounds despite playing with a broken nose, while Pope finished with a career-best 19 points and 10 boards. But on this afternoon in the Georgia Dome the list of Wildcat heroes also included Antoine Walker and Jeff Sheppard . It was Walker, in particular, who turned things around, keying a 14-3 spurt that took the Cats out of the danger zone and put them firmly on top. With the Cats holding a 33-31 lead with four minutes left in the first half, Walker dropped in a 10-foot jumper, then came up with a steal and assist that led to a Jared Prickett layup. Walker connected on a trey and a layup to give UK a 45-34 advantage and UK's lead at the half was a dozen points (50-38). Auburn closed the gap to nine points early in the sec-

ond half but a Sheppard three-pointer opened the gates for another big Kentucky explosion. Sheppard's bucket was followed in rapid succession by a McCarty 10-footer, a Tony Delk trey and a Walker dunk. When the damage had been done, UK's lead had ballooned to 65-46. The Cats were still leading by 18 (85-67) when Rodrick Rhodes hit a six-footer with just under four

minutes remaining. Then without warning, the Wildcats suddenly fell apart, committing a rash of turnovers against the desperate Tiger press. The UK miscues allowed the Tigers to score 11 unanswered points and trim the difference to 85-78. But a Delk leaner, two Sheppard free throws and a McCarty slam enabled the Cats to escape possible disaster.

Auburn	fg-a	3-pt	ft-a	rb	a	b	pf	tp
Chris Davis	5-12	0-0	7-7	7	1	1	4	17
Ray Donald	2-7	1-4	2-6	7	5	1	1	7
Pat Burke	5-11	0-1	3-4	6	2	3	2	13
Wes Flanigan	4-8	1-1	6-8	6	2	0	1	15
Moochie Norris	6-12	4-8	4-4	2	4	0	3	20
Jim Costner	1-1	0-0	0-0	2	0	0	1	2
Frank Williams	0-1	0-0	0-0	1	0	0	3	0
Lance Weems	2-6	2-5	1-2	4	1	0	4	7
Team rebounds				2				
Totals	25-58	8-19	23-31	37	15	5	19	81

Kentucky	fg-a	3-pt	ft-a	rb	a	b	pf	tp
Rodrick Rhodes	3-12	0-4	1-2	2	3	0	4	7
Walter McCarty	8-12	1-3	5-5	10	2	0	3	22
Andre Riddick	1-2	0-0	1-2	1	0	1	2	3
Tony Delk	3-13	1-5	0-2	5	3	1	4	7
Jeff Sheppard	5-7	2-3	2-2	4	1	0	4	14
Mark Pope	7-12	2-3	3-3	10	1	1	3	19
Jared Prickett	2-4	0-0	0-0	4	3	0	2	4
Anthony Epps	1-3	1-3	2-2	4	4	0	0	5
Antoine Walker	4-11	1-4	0-0	5	4	1	3	9
Chris Harrison	1-5	1-4	0-2	0	2	0	3	3
Team rebounds				4				
Totals	35-81	9-29	14-20	49	23	4	28	93

Auburn	38	43	—	81
Kentucky	50	43	—	93

Turnovers: Auburn 22, Kentucky 14
Technicals: none
Officials: Don Rutledge, David Dodge, Curtis Shaw
Attendance: 26,049

March 11

Georgia Dome • Atlanta, Ga.

Florida	72
Kentucky	**86**

"Once again, we shot well, and that's because we're really looking inside. When we do that, we're very strong."

— Rick Pitino

"We were in pretty good shape, then — boom — five possessions and you find yourself down 10 points. Kentucky is the kind of team that can do that to you."

— (Florida coach) Lon Kruger

Chalk up another one for the UK bench. With a host of starters struggling to find their game, Rick Pitino did what few other coaches can do ... he looked to his bench for deliverance. And what Pitino got was a game-deciding 55 points, 16 rebounds and 13 assists, which were more than enough to take care of the Gators for the third time this season. With subs Antoine Walker and Chris Harrison providing the heavy-duty artillery (they had 21 of the subs' 30 first-half points), the Cats were able to break open a tight game and earn a 26th trip to the SEC tourney championship game. The Cats trailed 14-11 when Walker's six-foot leaner jump-started the sluggish offense. Then after a Dan Williams free throw, Harrison knocked down a trey and a pull-up jumper to ignite a 16-1 run that put the Cats in front 29-16. Harrison's two buckets were followed by a Walker three-pointer, a trey and

layup by Mark Pope and another Harrison three-pointer. All the Gators had to offer in the way of a reply was a lone free throw by Dan Cross. UK led 45-30 at the half, with Walker's 13 leading the way. Kentucky's lead ranged between 11 and 18 points in the second half, until six points by Cross and two by

Greg Williams brought the Gators to within 10 at 71-61. But any thoughts of a Gator comeback were quickly snuffed by six straight UK points — two free throws apiece by Walker and Pope and a driving layup by Anthony Epps. Walker led the Wildcats in scoring with a career-high 21 points.

Florida	fg-a	3-pt	ft-a	rb	a	b	pf	tp
Brian Thompson	0-1	0-0	0-0	2	0	0	1	0
Andrew DeClercq	2-5	0-0	3-4	4	1	0	5	7
Dametri Hill	4-16	0-1	6-7	8	2	0	4	14
Greg Williams	4-9	1-3	2-2	5	2	0	3	11
Dan Cross	8-15	2-5	6-8	4	0	0	2	24
John Griffiths	1-1	0-0	0-0	0	0	0	0	2
Jason Anderson	4-6	0-0	1-3	5	3	1	1	9
LeRon Williams	2-3	0-0	0-0	3	0	0	1	4
Dan Williams	0-0	0-0	1-4	0	1	0	0	1
Tony Mickens	0-0	0-0	0-0	0	0	1	0	0
Damen Maddox	0-0	0-0	0-0	0	0	0	0	0
Team rebounds				5				
Totals	**25-56**	**3-9**	**19-28**	**36**	**9**	**2**	**17**	**72**

Kentucky	fg-a	3-pt	ft-a	rb	a	b	pf	tp
Rodrick Rhodes	3-9	2-5	0-0	3	5	0	2	8
Walter McCarty	1-1	0-0	2-2	1	1	1	5	4
Andre Riddick	1-2	0-0	0-1	1	0	1	2	2
Tony Delk	4-12	1-5	3-4	0	3	2	2	12
Jeff Sheppard	2-5	1-1	0-0	4	0	0	3	5
Mark Pope	5-6	2-3	4-5	8	1	5	5	16
Jared Prickett	1-2	0-0	0-0	3	2	2	2	2
Anthony Epps	3-4	0-1	2-2	0	7	0	3	8
Antoine Walker	7-10	3-3	4-4	5	2	0	2	21
Chris Harrison	3-4	2-3	0-0	0	1	0	2	8
Scott Padgett	0-1	0-1	0-0	0	0	0	0	0
Team rebounds				2				
Totals	**30-56**	**11-22**	**15-18**	**27**	**22**	**11**	**26**	**86**

Florida	30	42	—	72
Kentucky	45	41	—	86

Turnovers: Florida 14, Kentucky 11
Technicals: none
Officials: John Clougherty, Gary Boudreaux, Rusty Herring
Attendance: 28,966

1995
March 12
Georgia Dome • Atlanta, Ga.

Arkansas
Kentucky

OT 93
    95

> "It was an interesting game in a lot of ways. We showed great courage and character in coming back against a team like Arkansas. This is one of the proudest moments I've had in coaching."
>
> — Rick Pitino

> "Coach told me that I'm no longer a freshman, that I had to step up and take my game to a different level if we were going to do well in the tournament. So that's what I did."
>
> — Antoine Walker

L ike a courageous boxer who appeared to be down for the count, UK twice found the strength to pull itself up off the canvas and stop the Razorbacks to capture the SEC tourney title for the fourth straight year. This game, perhaps the best in all post-season play, featured enough drama, thrills and heartbreak to last an entire season. From the heroics of Anthony Epps, Mark Pope and Corliss Williamson to the down-in-the-depths despair of Rodrick Rhodes and Corey Beck, this was nothing less than top-notch theater played out in front of 30,000 fans and a regional television audience. In every way, it was as good as college basketball gets. To win the school's 19th SEC Tournament crown, the Cats had to overcome a 19-point first-half deficit and then a nine-point deficit in overtime. The Hogs, led by

the long-range gunning of Scotty Thurman and the surprisingly strong play of Darnell Robinson, blitzed the Cats, opening a 35-16 lead inside the game's first 10 minutes. During that span, Kentucky contributed to its own troubles by turning the ball over 10 times against the pressing, aggressive Arkansas defense. But somehow the Cats managed to fight back. A short jumper by Chris Harrison and an eight-footer by Rhodes started the Cats on their road to recovery. Back-to-back buckets by Jeff Sheppard, a 15-footer by Tony Delk, four points by Rhodes, a slam by tourney MVP Antoine Walker and two Jared Prickett free throws, countered by just eight Arkansas points, pulled UK to within 42-34 with 3:38 left in the frenetic first half. Both teams sizzled from the field in those opening 20 minutes, with

Kentucky hitting 16 of 25 shots for 64 percent and Arkansas hitting 19 of 35 for 54.3 percent. The Hogs were especially accurate from three-point range, connecting on eight of 14. UK trailed throughout the second half, and didn't catch up until a Walker tip-in and a three-point play by Walter McCarty made it 78-78 with 2:03 remaining. After Williamson scored on a driving layup, Pope dropped in a pair of free throws with 22 seconds left to tie it at 80-80. UK gained possession with 5.5 ticks left, at which time Rick Pitino inserted Rhodes into the game with the single-minded purpose of taking the ball to the basket. Pitino's piece of strategy worked, with Rhodes drawing a foul from Clint McDaniel. But Rhodes misfired on both freebies, sending the game into overtime. Given a reprieve, the Hogs immedi-